Ecclesiologia, or the Doctrine Concerning the Church

By Revere Franklin Weidner

Works of Revere Franklin Weidner

ECCLESIOLOGIA, OR THE DOCTRINE
CONCERNING THE CHURCH
REVERE FRANKLIN WEIDNER

JUST & SINNER
WATSEKA, IL 60970

WWW.JUSTANDSINNER.COM

ISBN 10: 069229936X
ISBN 13: 978-0692299364

TABLE OF CONTENTS

INTRODUCTION

Revere Franklin Weidner is one of the brightest lights in American Lutheranism, although he remains relatively unknown in the present day. In addition to being a vastly prolific writer, he wrote books concerning virtually every theological discipline. He has a multivolume Dogmatics series, several Biblical commentaries, and two volumes on the Biblical Theology of the Old and New Testaments. Weidner also wrote in the areas of ethics, historical theology, and practical theology.

When one reads the works of Weidner, it becomes quickly apparent that he did not seek to be an original thinker. Rather, Weidner desired to bring historic Confessional Lutheran Theology, in the vein of the seventeenth century dogmaticians, to nineteenth century America. Thus, his works are largely summaries of the older dogmaticians. Weidner also drew on contemporary writers, from Lutheran and other church traditions. He is most highly indebted to his eminent teacher Charles Porterfield Krauth, and the German theologian Ernst Luthardt. He rarely takes credit for his own ideas, and often attributes them to the lectures of Krauth.

Of the theologians of the Confessional revival in America of the nineteenth and early twentieth century, many important figures remain unknown. Aside from C.F.W. Walther, Franz Pieper, Wilhelm Loehe, and Charles Krauth, most of these writers have been lost in the annuls of history. Of the many great figures that characterized this rich period of theological development, Weidner is perhaps the most prolific. Thus, this series is an attempt to bring the name of this significant theologian back into contemporary theological conversations.

We live in an era where scholastic Lutheranism has been largely forgotten due to the influence of later twentieth century theological development. These developments sought to go back to the writings of Luther himself, devoid of seventeenth century interpretation of those writings. Within this school of thought, prominent in the "Radical Lutheran" school of Gerhard Forde and Steven Paulson, it is argued that there is a profound discontinuity between Luther's Gospel-centric theology and the dry scholasticism of the seventeenth century. In contrast to this, dogmatic theology can rightly be seen as the natural outgrowth and systematizing of Luther's own theological system. While Luther himself was no systematic theologian, he applauded the efforts of Melanchthon for putting Reformation theology within a Dogmatic framework. Now, in the twenty-first century, we are placed in a theological quandary: shall we abandon the Lutheran heritage in favor of newer theological schools of thought which seek to go back to the "real Luther," or should we recapture our rich dogmatic heritage? This series is an attempt to give an answer to this dilemma by providing theological texts which speak just as profoundly to the world and the church's problems in the twenty-first century as they did at the end of the nineteenth. May Weidner's words help the church to "grow in the grace and the knowledge of our Lord and Savior Jesus Christ" (2 Pet. 3:18).

Note on This Volume
This work is taken from lectures he gave to Weidner's seminary students. The original volume appeared in outline form, rather than the typical prose one would find in a systematic theology volume. For easier reading, I have taken the book out of outline form, and have made the sections into paragraphs. Because of that, some of the wording and structure might seem awkward, but I tried to stay as close to the author's original words as possible. Apart from occasional additions to help the flow of the text, or to make fragments into full sentences, the words are Weidner's rather than my own.

Jordan Cooper
Watseka, IL
2014

THE ESSENTIAL CHARACTER AND ATTRIBUTES OF THE CHURCH

The whole field of Dogmatics and Polemics is in some shape or other involved in the doctrine concerning the Church. It is the great question of the day, and to give a complete Bibliography would require a volume.

The fact of the establishment of the Church by the outpouring of the Holy Ghost, as well as the Apostolic doctrine of the spiritual body of Christ, if compared with the actual character and condition of the Apostolic Church, teaches us that in the Church, *i.e.*, in the assembly or communion of the people of Jesus Christ, the *spiritual* essence is to be distinguished from that which is actually developed by experience and presented in it (*Luthardt*).

According to its spiritual essence the Church is the collection or assembly of believers who are united in the Holy Ghost with Christ their invisible Head, and with one another. It is also the institution which gathers men by the visible means of grace and administers these means in the service of Christ (*Luthardt*).

This spiritual nature of the Church's essence is shared also by its attributes of unity, holiness, apostolicity, and catholicity. Consequently only those are in truth members of the Church who are participants in this, its spiritual essence (*Luthardt*). But inasmuch as the Church has the fulfilling of a historical vocation in the world, it must become in its actual development an external organization rightly constituted, so that to the Church in this sense belong all those who are part of the outward organism (*Luthardt*).

It is the laying stress upon the one side, upon this outward organism,—or on the other side, upon the spiritual essence of the Church,—which makes and marks the distinction between the Roman and the Evangelical Lutheran conception of the Church, with which latter view the whole Protestant world, with greater or less consistency, supposes itself to coincide (*Krauth*).

I. THE SCRIPTURE DOCTRINE

Three Hebrew words are used in the O.T. to designate the congregation of the people, *qahal,* "assembly," *edha,* "congregation," and *miqra,* "convocation." The first two occur together in Ex. 12:6 and Num. 14:5. The Septuagint (Greek O.T.) uses mainly the word *ecclesia* to translate *qahal* (some 70 times), but never uses it to translate the other two words.

It uses the word *synagogue* for the most part (some 100 times) to translate *edha,* and about 25 times to translate *qahal.* The authorised English Version shows the same lack of consistent rendering, but the Revised Version is more consistent, translating as above. Although the Septuagint put *synagogue* for *edha,* and as a rule *ecclesia* for *qahal,* it is difficult to decide whether any distinction can be drawn in meaning as used in the O.T.

Later Judaism, according to Schuerer, seems to have made a distinction, *edha,* the *synagogue,* being the actual congregation as constituted and existing in some one place, and *qahal,* the *ecclesia,* on the other hand, being the ideal church of Israel, the assembly of those called by God to salvation. It is thus easy to understand why the word *ecclesia* displaces the word *synagogue* in Christian circles, and in the N.T. we find *ecclesia* only twice applied to the O.T. Church (Acts 7:38; Heb. 2:12), the word *synagogue* everywhere else designating the congregation of the Jews (Acts 13:43; James 2:2) or their place of assembly, save in Rev. 2:9; 3:9.

Just as in the O.T., the people of Israel are characterized as "the assembly" (*qahal*) "of the Lord" (Num. 16:3), or "of God" (Neh. 13:1), so our Lord not without due reason designates the new society of which He is the Founder, *the Church* (*ecclesia, i.e., qahal,* Matt. 16:18), the N.T. people of God thus corresponding with the O.T. assembly, as fruit corresponds with the blossom, or antitype with type.

The word *ecclesia* is used in the N.T. in its three distinct stages of meaning:

1) In its *classical* meaning, as an assembly of the people, possessed of the rights of citizenship, convened for the transaction of public affairs. So used in Acts 19:32, 39, 41.

2) In its *Jewish* sense, referring to the O.T. Church, as in Acts 7:38; Heb. 2:12.

3) In its distinctively *Christian* sense.

The origin of the word *Church* is somewhat uncertain. It seems best to trace it (and Danish *kirke*, Swedish *kyrka*, Icelandic *kirkja*, Dutch *kerk*, German *kirche*) to the Greek word *kuriakon*, a church, neuter of *kuriakos*, belonging to the Lord, from the Greek *kurios*, the Lord.

The usage of the word *ecclesia* (in its Christian sense) in the N.T. is two-fold:

I. It denotes the entire assembly of saints (qahal), all who are in fellowship with Christ—the entire Church universal. This is its primary meaning.

This is clear from the O.T. use of the word, and from the fundamental statement of Christ in Matt. 16:18, "Upon this rock I will build my Church." So Acts 5:11; 9:31; 12:1, 5; 20:28; Gal. 1:13; 1 Cor. 6:4; 10:32; 11:22; 12:28; 14:4, 5, 12; 15:9; Rom. 16:23; Col. 1:18, 24; Eph. 1:22; 3:10, 21; 5:23, 24, 25, 27, 29, 32; Phil. 3:6; Heb. 12:23; 1 Tim. 3:5, 15; etc.

II. The name is given to congregations confined to particular places.

1) To a single congregation, Acts 8:1; 11:22 26; 13:1; 14:23; 15:3, 4, 22; 18:22; etc.

2) To congregations at various places, using the plural,— *churches*: Acts 15:41; 16:5; 1 Thess. 2:14; 2 Thess. 1:4; Gal. 1:2, 22; 1 Cor. 7:17; 11:16; 14:33, 34; 16:1, 19; 2 Cor. 8:1, 18, 19, 23, 24; 11:8, 28; 12:13; Rom. 16:16; etc.

The Teaching of Jesus

Our Lord makes the first use of the term (Matt. 16:18), and by the term *church* is meant the entire communion or assembly of N.T. believers, which was to consist, according to Matt. 18:17, of individual congregations or churches.

The true doctrine concerning the essential character, *i.e.,* the spiritual nature, of the Church is given us in Christ's teaching concerning the Kingdom of God, as recorded in Matt. 13:1–52. This chapter exhausts generically the doctrine concerning the Church.

The parable of the Sower (Matt. 13:3–9, 18–23) teaches us that the Church is generated by the Word of God rightly received in faith; The parable of the Tares (Matt. 13:24–30, 36–43) teaches us the mixed condition of the Church as a visible institution, and the impossibility of having on earth a perfectly pure visible Church. The seed in this parable are men, not doctrines,—yet they are such men as the doctrines they embody make them—wheat and tares; The parable of the Mustard Seed (Matt. 13:31, 32) emphasizes its little beginning, its steady progress, and its final mighty consummation; The parable of the Leaven (Matt. 13:33) teaches its self-diffusing manner of working and its all-assimilating power; The parable of the Treasure hidden in the field (Matt. 13:44) sets forth its intrinsic preciousness as found, in the providence of God, by those who were not searching for it; The parable of the Pearl of great price (Matt. 13:45, 46) teaches the incomparable glory of the Kingdom of God as found by the earnest seeker; The parable of the Draw-net (Matt. 13:47–50) teaches that there will be a final complete sundering of the evil from the good after the all-comprehending work of the Church.

We must distinguish between the Church as it exists in its visible form as an actual society of professing Christians, and the Kingdom of God in its final consummation. In Matt. 16:18, 19, where both terms ("Church", "Kingdom of God") occur, the Kingdom of God is the future and heavenly counterpart of the Church on earth.

With reference to *time*, Jesus describes His Kingdom under a *two-fold* aspect:

1) As already begun and existing in the present (Matt. 12:28). It coincides with His appearance (Matt 11:11, 12); its starting point is with John the Baptist (Luke 16:16); it has a real existence (Luke 17:21), and one can enter into it through regeneration (John 3:3, 5).

2) As something future (Matt. 6:10, "thy Kingdom come"; 16:28; Luke 21:31; 22:29, 30; etc.).

With reference to the *nature* of the Kingdom:

1) It is a *divine order of things*, realized through Christ the Redeemer. It is not of this world, not to be supported by force (John 18:36); it is distinct from the civil order of the world (Matt. 11:12); its object is to give "unto God the things that are God's," and "unto Cæsar the things that are Cæsar's" (Matt. 22:17–21); the Church has no part in questions of mere earthly law or

equity, and Christ declines to be a Judge or decider in the sphere of civil law (Luke 12:13, 14).

As the Kingdom is being realized through Christ, it is His Kingdom (Matt. 16:18; 13:41), and the unveiling of it is the revelation of the Son of Man (Luke 17:22–24, 30).

The development of the Kingdom is *from within*. It does not consist essentially in outward ordinances, but is internal and spiritual (Luke 17:20, 21), "the Kingdom of God cometh not with observation," *i.e.*, with outward show, in such a manner that it can be watched with the eyes.

The essential constituent of the Church is *personal communion* with Christ, a communion on which our Lord dwells with special fullness in His last recorded discourse (John 15:1–17:26). The relation of the Church to Christ is that of branches to the vine (John 15:5), so intimate that the unity of Person within the Godhead is offered as its parallel, "that they may all be one, even as thou, Father, art in me, and I in thee, that they also may be in us" (John 17:21), "I in them, and thou in me, that they may be perfected into one" (17:23), and the Savior closes with the words, "and I in them" (17:26).

As a Kingdom of God *on earth*, it is a fellowship of men united for the possession of a common good, or to exercise some common action (the parable of the Tares, Matt. 13:24–30, 37–43; of the great Marriage Feast, Matt. 22:2–14; of the Ten Virgins, Matt. 25:1–13; of the Laborers in the Vineyard, 20:1–16; etc.).

It is to embrace *humanity as a whole*, and the gospel is to be preached to the whole world (Matt. 13:38; 24:14, 28:19). Jesus has other sheep (John 10:16); He invites them from the highways and lanes (Matt. 22:10; Luke 14:21).

It comprises *heaven and earth*, likewise the coming periods of the world, both before and after the Judgment. Not only does it exist on earth (Matt. 12:28; Luke 17:20, 21), and all nations shall receive it (Matt. 13:32; 8:11; 24:14), but its prototype is the *kingdom of God in heaven* (Matt. 6:10; 5:10, 12; 6:33). It embraces *all the periods of man's history*, from Christ onwards (Matt. 4:17; Luke 17:20; Matt. 28:20); There are two chief periods of God's kingdom which are separated by the epoch of Judgment: 1) *this age* or *œon*, during which the Kingdom of God and of the world exist together,—a mixture of good and evil, and 2) *the age* (or æon) *which is to come* (Matt. 12:32), when the Kingdom of God shall exist by itself in its purity and perfection ("When the righteous shall shine forth as the sun in the Kingdom of their Father," (Matt. 13:40–43). In Mark 10:30 and Luke 20:34, 35, these two periods are designated: 1) as "this time," "this world" (or age) and 2) "the age to come," "that world" (or age).

This Kingdom which has a gradual development among men extends *beyond the world of men*, and comprehends *the good angels*. They are *His* angels (Matt. 16:27; 13:41; 24:31), and are regarded as members of His Kingdom, and now in heaven do God's will. Therefore the Kingdom of God already exists in heaven in its truth and reality, entirely setting aside its existence or continuance on earth.

From the fellowship of believers with Christ necessarily follows the spiritual and internal fellowship of believers with one another (John 15:12, 17; 17:21).

In order to establish His Church, our Savior gathered His disciples about Him, promised them the Holy Spirit, gave them the commandment that the gospel should be preached in all the world to every creature, instituted the Sacrament of Baptism and of the Lord's Supper, gave them the principles underlying Church discipline, leaving free all merely human external ordinances, limiting them only to a general conformity to the letter and spirit of His teaching.

The Church as developing itself from within, depends for its growth on the *communication of the life of Christ*, and is *founded, maintained and guided by Him.* It is Christ who builds His Church on the rock Peter (Matt. 16:18), and He will quicken and guide it unto the end of this world (Matt. 28:20); even to the smallest gathering of His people in His name, there He will be present in all authority and with all power (Matt. 18:19, 20); the Church being founded and guided by Him, has an immovable existence (Matt. 16:18) and a sure and firm continuance, and there is nothing on earth or in Hades that shall prevail against it (Matt. 16:18). The special signs which give manifestation of the existence of the Church are the preaching of the Word of Christ, and the administration of the Sacrament of Baptism and of the Lord s Supper.

The Word of Christ is the authentic testimony of God's Son (John 3:11), the Word of God (John 12:48–50; 14:10; 7:16; 17:6); it is the spirit and the life (John 6:63); by this word faith is brought about (John 17:20; 5:24); it is the truth which sets free from sin and sanctifies (John 8:31, 32, 36; 17:17, 19); by this word unbelievers will be judged at the last day (John 12:48). Thus the Word of Christ is essentially the basis or groundwork of God's Kingdom on earth. Men possess it only through Christ.

From Matt. 28:19; Mark 16:16; John 3:5 we learn that *baptism*, in addition to the word, is also the way to Christ,—and for this reason the Lord caused His disciples to baptize (John 4:1, 2).

The institution of the Lord's Supper took place at the last Passover meal (Matt. 26:26–29; Mark 14:22–25; Luke 22:14–20, and although they were sitting at the table at the time, we must carefully distinguish it from the Passover meal itself, for both Luke (22:20) and Paul (1 Cor. 11:25), most distinctly say *after supper*. Just as the Word and Baptism are connected in bringing about *faith* and an *entrance* into the Kingdom of God, so the Word and the Lord's Supper are connected in strengthening the faith of believers, and in continually quickening and confirming a spiritual communion of love.

Thus the *three means of grace* are the inexhaustible and life-giving groundwork of the Church on earth, as a community of believers, but only in this age or æon. The Church will continue in the future age or æon, but not in the same form or shape, for evidently Baptism and the Lord's Supper can only remain entirely the same so long as the material elements are entirely the same (Matt. 26:29; Mark 14:25; Luke 22:18).

Christ also clearly teaches us that in this age or æon, as the Church exists on earth, there is a two-fold feature, which we cannot overlook:

1) In the Church there is a mingling of genuine and non-genuine members. See especially the Parable of the Tares (Matt. 13:24, 30, 37–43). Not even all those who call upon the name of the Lord are members of His Kingdom (Matt. 7:21).

2) There are distinctive grades among the genuine members of the Church. Some are eminent in activity and take the lead, while others become recipients of their ministry and guidance. Our Lord saw that Peter was the natural leader of the Twelve (John 1:42; Matt. 16:18, 19; Luke 22:32; John 21:15). The Apostles themselves as a body, are appointed as the teachers and guides of other believers (Acts 1:8; John 15:27; Matt. 28:19; John 20:21–23).

The gradual development of the Church on earth and its final consummation are presented in the form of three *chief epochs*:

1) *The first epoch* is the destruction of the Jewish State and Church.

a) The Kingdom of God could make its appearance only in Israel (John 4:22; Matt. 10:5, 6, etc.), and in it the Church first grew up, although it is destined to embrace all nations.

b) The opposition of the Jews necessitated another course of development, and resulted in a judgment upon Israel as a nation. Our Savior most distinctly declared this judgment, again and again (the Parable of the Wicked Husbandmen, Matt. 21:33–45; Mark 12:1–12; Luke 20:9–19; of the Marriage Feast, Matt. 22:1–14; especially in the prophecy concerning the Destruction of Jerusalem, Matt. 24:5–28; Mark 13:5–23; Luke 21:8–24). The destruction of Jerusalem has become an epoch in the development of the Church. This epoch had a two-fold character—it was a judgment upon Israel, and a deliverance for the Christian Church.

2) The *second epoch* is the period of the spread of Christianity among all nations.

a) The progress of God's Kingdom on earth is left to the Church and her activities.

b) The Parable of "the Seed growing Secretly" (Mark 4:26–29) teaches us that the Lord especially interferes only at the beginning and at the end, in the sowing and in the reaping, that having planted the growing corn, the Church develops by the means that He as the Head of the Church has entrusted to her.

c) This course of development of the Church, through its manifold phases, is largely conditioned by the relation which the Church bears to her Head and Lord, even to Christ Himself,—on the zeal and faithfullness of believers.

d) This period has already lasted longer than seemed likely at the beginning, and may end in the near future, for the last epoch will surely come to pass.

3) The *last epoch*, the consummation of the age (Matt. 13:39, 40; 24:3; 28:20), begins with the day of Judgment (Matt. 24:29–31, 37–39; Luke 21:25–27). It is ushered in by the *Parousia* or the Second Advent of the Lord (Matt. 24:27, 39; Luke 17:24, 30). With this Parousia a *continuous Judgment* in the Church is connected, a Judgment distinguished from the universal Judgment, for it severs

those who are true believers from those who only outwardly profess to be Christians. This is what is meant by the marriage feast (Matt. 22:2–14), to this marriage feast the five wise virgins entered (Matt. 25:10), this is the redemption spoken of in Luke 21:28. The final or universal Judgment follows at the end of time, at the close of the consummation of the age, at the end of the world as a thing in time.

Although the assembly of God (Neh. 13:1), called also the assembly of the Lord (Deut. 23:1), existed in O.T. times, nevertheless we may say that the Church of Christ (Matt. 16:18; Rom. 16:16) was properly founded on the Day of Pentecost, by no other means than the outpouring of the Holy Ghost, as a token and proof of its essentially spiritual nature.

The Teaching of the Apostles

The teaching of Peter. Those who wish to connect themselves with the Church of Christ must be baptized in the name of Jesus Christ unto the remission of sins (Acts 2:38, 41; 10:48), and the Church is bound together and grows by believers participating in the teaching of the Apostles, by brotherly fellowship with one another, by partaking of the Lord's Supper, and by uniting in common prayer (Acts 2:42).

As a house as a whole consists of different parts, so the Church of God is being continually built up of individual believers who are living stones in this spiritual house (1 Pet. 2:5). The Church is represented as a holy, priestly people of God, "an elect race, a royal priesthood, a holy nation, a people for God's own possession," who are to "show forth the excellencies of Him who called them out of darkness into His marvelous light" (1 Pet. 2:9, 10).

Christians are called "an elect race" inasmuch as God has *chosen* them out of the kingdom of the world to be His own; they are a "royal priesthood," because the Church is a *kingdom* of which all the members are priests (1 Pet. 2:5; Rev. 1:6; 5:10), who serve the King with spiritual sacrifices; these spiritual sacrifices which are acceptable to God through Jesus Christ (1 Pet. 2:5), are: a spiritual sacrifice *a)* of their bodies (Rom. 12:1),—including true self-denial (Heb. 13:16; Phil. 4:18) and the taking up of one's cross daily (Luke 9:23), and *b)* of prayer and praise (Heb. 13:15; Rev. 8:3,

4); they are called a "holy nation" (Ex. 19:6; Eph. 5:25–27), because God has "chosen us in Christ, before the foundation of the world, *that we should be holy* and without blemish before Him" (Eph. 1:4); they are "a people for God's own possession" (Ex. 19:5; Deut. 7:6; Mal. 3:17; but especially Isa. 43:21), for to this end Christ died, that "He might redeem from all iniquity, and purify unto Himself *a people for His own possession,* zealous of good works" (Tit. 2:14).

Israel was once the Church of God, but now the Christian Church, consisting of believing Jews and converted Gentiles, has become the Church of God (1 Pet. 2:5, 9, 10; 4:17); Christ as the Head of the Church is both Shepherd and Bishop (overseer) of the souls of believers (1 Pet. 2:25). As a shepherd Christ nourishes, strengthens, and feeds; as a bishop he searcheth and seeketh out His sheep and disciplines them.

The teaching of Paul.

The doctrine of the Church is fully developed by Paul in his four great doctrinal Epistles (Gal., 1 Cor., 2 Cor. Rom.) and in his Pastoral Epistles, but most fully stated in his profound Epistle to the Ephesians. Although it would be interesting to develop his teaching in each of his epistles separately, it will be best to give it in its totality.

The use of the word Ecclesia. Paul uses the word *Church* in its three-fold sense:

1) As designating the assembly of Church members in a *single congregation* in any definite place (Rom. 16:1, 5; 1 Cor. 1:2; 4:17; 11:18; etc. Often in the plural, Rom. 16:4, 16; 1 Cor. 7:17; 11:16; 16:1, 19; etc.).

2) As designating the collective community of Christians, the *visible Church Universal,* "all that call upon the name of our Lord Jesus Christ in every place," 1 Cor. 1:2 (1 Cor. 10:32; 12:28; 15:9; Gal. 1:13; Phil. 3:6; 1 Tim. 3:2, 15).

3) As designating the *ideal* Church, the *invisible Church Universal* (so especially in Ephesians; also Col. 1:18, 24; 2:19; 3:15; etc.).

The origin of the Church. In Christ Himself the Church originates. It is the emanation of His life.

1) Paul regards baptism as that act by which the Christian participates in the Holy Spirit, and is put into a real living

fellowship with Christ (Rom. 6:3–5; Gal. 3:27, 28; 1 Cor. 1:2; 6:11, 19);

2) By this living fellowship all are equally connected with the living center, even Christ, and so have become one organism, "one body in Christ, and severally members one of another" (Rom. 12:5), "for in one Spirit were we all baptized into one body" (1 Cor. 12:13).

3) The Christian community was in its origin a house-congregation (Acts 1:13–15; 2:46; 5:42; 17:7; 20:8, 20; 1 Cor. 16:15, 19; Rom. 16:5; Col. 4:15; Philemon 2; etc.). The Church in a city was composed of a number of these house-congregations and for the purpose of direction and administration the unit was the city-congregation and not the house-congregation (Acts 13:1; 20:28), and for this reason Paul always directs his letters to the Church of the city and not to the house-congregation (1 Cor. 1:1, 2).

A distinction is drawn between the *actual* Church and the *ideal* Church:

The *actual* Church is composed of members who are still alive at the time of speaking, and includes individuals of various degrees of imperfection. It is the actual Church to which reproof and blame are addressed (1 Cor. 1:10; 3:1; 5:1; Gal. 3:1–3; etc.); the actual visible Church does not only contain many *teachers* whose work consists simply in gathering "wood, hay, and stubble" (1 Cor. 3:12, 15), but many of the professing members of the Church are but "wood, hay, and stubble;" the actual visible Church is "the great house which contains not only vessels of gold and silver, but also of wood and earth; and some unto honor, and some unto dishonor" (2 Tim. 2:20). Many are members of the Church externally, and "name the name of the Lord," but do not depart from unrighteousness (2 Tim. 2:19).

The *ideal* Church is the body of true believers, in living fellowship with Christ, who, although ever capable of progress and higher perfection (Eph. 4:12–16, are washed by baptism from every stain (1 Cor. 6:11; Heb. 10:14; 1 John 3:9), and are holy, even *saints* (Rom. 8:27; 1 Cor. 6:1, 2; 2 Cor. 1:1; Eph. 1:1; etc.). It is this *ideal* Church which shall judge the world (1 Cor. 6:2), which is sanctified and cleansed "by the washing of water with the word ... the glorious Church, not having spot or wrinkle or any such thing, ... holy and without blemish" (Eph. 5:26, 27).

The Ideal Church is spoken of as a Building.

Although Paul in 1 Cor. 6:19 regards the individual believer as "a temple of the Holy Ghost" (possibly also in 1 Cor. 3:16 and 2 Cor. 6:16, but it is better to refer *temple* in these pages also to the *Church*) we find that in 1 Cor. 3:9–15 he compares the Church to a building, a *spiritual house*, whose foundation is Jesus Christ, on which he and all ministers of the Word have continually to build (1 Cor. 3:9, 16; 2 Cor. 6:16; 1 Tim. 3:15; Eph. 2:21, 22; Heb. 3:6). This agrees with Christ's own statement, "I will *build* my Church" (Matt. 16:18), and with Peter's teaching that the Church of God is composed or built up of individual believers who are *living* stones in the spiritual house, resting on Jesus Christ, the chief cornerstone (1 Pet. 2:5–8).

In Eph. 2:20–22 the whole Church is regarded as a "holy temple," "a habitation of God," the foundation being the apostles and prophets, Christ Jesus Himself being the chief cornerstone (Eph. 2:20), in which building each individual Christian or congregation, "fitly framed together," each fitting into his proper place, and the whole builded together," *i.e.*, held together by Christ, "groweth into a holy temple in the Lord" (Eph. 2:21, 22).

The Ideal Church is spoken of as a Body.

This is the figure which Paul seems to prefer (Rom. 12:5; 1 Cor. 6:15; 10:17; 12:12–27; Eph. 1:22, 23; 4:4, 12, 16; 5:23; Col. 1:18, 24; 2:19). The Church is "the body of Christ" (Eph. 1:23; 4:12; 5:23, 30; Col. 1:18, 24; 2:19), a name "infinite in depth and yet transparently clear, both bodily and spiritual, objective and subjective, open and mysterious, at the same time" (*Delitzsch*).

In 1 Cor. 12:12–27 we have one of the most beautiful illustrations in human language developing the *organic unity* of Christ's one body and the manifold offices and mutual dependences of its many members. Compare also Rom. 12:4, 5, where the same thought is presented. Paul also emphasizes the fact that we are and become one body, when we partake in the body of Christ, in the Lord's Supper (1 Cor. 10:16, 17). Sometimes Paul identifies Christ with the whole body, "for in one Spirit were we all baptized into one body" (1 Cor. 12:13), for "ye are the body of Christ, and severally members thereof" (1 Cor. 12:27).

In his later Epistles, Paul emphasizes the thought that Christ is the head of the body, its all-pervading soul, the source of its life, for God has given "Him to be head over all things to the Church, which is his body, the fullness of him that filleth all in all" (Eph. 1:22, 23). See also Eph. 4:15; 5:23, 24; Col. 1:18; 2:19.

In the essential unity which pervades the body all distinctions are abrogated. There is one perfectly similar communion of spirit with God,—"there is one body, and one Spirit"—(Eph. 4:4, 12); there can be neither Jew nor Greek, neither bond nor free, neither male nor female, "for ye all are one in Christ Jesus" (Gal. 3:28),— Christ has broken down the middle wall of partition between Jew and Gentile (Eph. 2:13–18).

The Ideal Church is spoken of as a Bride.

The comparison of the Church to a *bride*, "a pure virgin," is first met with in 2 Cor. 11:2, "for I espoused you to one husband, that I might present you as a pure virgin to Christ." The Church is this *virgin*; the presentation occurs at the *Parousia*, when Christ appears as bridegroom to fetch home the bride (Matt. 25:1–13; Rev. 19:7–9). This is a great mystery, says St. Paul (Eph. 5:32). The Church is the bride of Christ; the two are one body, just as man and wife are one body (Eph. 5:23–32).

The Church of the living God is the pillar and ground of the truth (1 Tim. 3:15). A *pillar*, because having the Spirit of God (even the Spirit of truth), the Church supports and preserves divine truth; the *ground* or *stay* or *bulwark* of truth, for if there were no Church there would be no witness, no bulwark, no basis, nothing whereon acknowledged truth could rest. Note, then, the true office and vocation of the Church.

As the Church depends on the means of grace (the Word, Baptism, and Lord's Supper) for her existence and perpetuation, there is necessary a ministry of these means:"the ministry of the Word" (Acts 6:4; 1 Tim. 4:13, 15; 2 Tim. 4:2), "the ministration of the Spirit" (2 Cor. 3:8), of which ministry there were manifold organs (apostles, prophets, evangelists, pastors, teachers, Eph. 4:11). Compare 1 Cor. 12:28.

The teaching of John.

Owing to the peculiar character of John's mind, the idea of the Church is not distinctly brought forward, though its existence is implied (3 John 6, 9). With him there is, like with St. Paul, a *visible* and an *invisible* Church (1 John 2:19). Believers have fellowship with the Father and the Son (1 John 1:3), and with one another (1 John 3:7). Believers are brethren in virtue of being partakers in the new birth from God (1 John 4:20, 21 compared with 5:1, 2). Love to God (1 John 3:16–18; 2 John 9) and a right confession of faith (1 John 2:23; 4:2; 2 John 7–11) causes this fellowship to be both inward and outward. It would be interesting to develop St. John's doctrine of the Church as given in the Apocalypse, but this would lead us beyond our present purpose.

THE CHURCH DOCTRINE

I. *The Ancient Catholic Church*

From the beginning two aspects of the Church have always been recognized, 1) its inner and spiritual essence, and 2) its outward organism as actually developed.

The early Church laid stress upon the historical actuality of the Church, and the doctrine of the Church was developed on this basis. This development, in the Ante-Nicene Period, can be conveniently discussed in connection with three great names, each separated from the other by an interval of more than half a century, and each marking a distinct stage in its progress,— Ignatius of Antioch (martyr 107 A. D., or 115 A. D.), Irenæus of Lyons (martyr 202 A. D.), and Cyprian of Carthage (martyr 258 A. D.).

Ignatius lays emphasis upon the bishop or head-pastor of the congregation as constituting the visible *center of unity* in the congregation. The episcopacy of Ignatius is, however, strictly congregational,—local, not diocesan, and purely governmental, valued mainly as a means of securing good discipline and promoting harmonious working in the Church. Submission to the bishop was considered as a *doctrine* of the Church, and the bishop was regarded as the *vicar* of Christ.

In his letter to Polycarp, bishop of Smyrna, Ignatius writes: "Maintain thine office with all care, in things temporal as well as spiritual" (*cap.* 1); "let nothing be done without thy consent, neither do thou anything without the approval of God" (*cap.* 4). In the same letter addressing the people, he adds: "Give heed to your bishop, that God also may give heed to you" (cap. 6).

In his letter to the Ephesians, Ignatius says: "It is evident that we should look upon the bishop as we would upon the Lord Himself" (cap. 6). To the Smyrnæans he writes: "See that ye all follow the bishop, even as Jesus Christ does the Father" ... "Let no man do anything connected with the Church without the bishop" ... "Wherever the bishop is found, there let the people be; even as, wherever Christ is, there is the *catholic* Church" (cap. 8). (With Zahn and Lightfoot we accept the genuineness of the shorter Greek recension of the Ignatian Epistles.)

With Irenæus, bishop of Lyons, two generations later, the aspect of the episcopal office has changed. Heresies everywhere abound, and the believer asks for some decisive test. Irenæus points to the Church as the sole depositary of apostolical doctrine, and the episcopate is by him regarded not so much as the *center of ecclesiastical unity* (as by Ignatius), but rather as the *depositary of Apostolic tradition.*

Irenæus *Against Heresies*: "The tradition derived from the apostles," ... "the faith preached to men," "comes down to our times by means of the succession of the bishops,"... "inasmuch as the apostolical tradition has been preserved continuously." (III. cap. 3).

To confirm this teaching that there was one unchanging rule of faith, preserved by infallible tradition, through an unbroken succession of bishops from the time of the apostles, attempts were now made (especially by Hegesippus and Irenæus in the second century, and by Eusebius and others in the fourth and following centuries) to construct lists of bishops especially in Rome, in order to establish this continuity. With this view of Irenæus both Hegisippus (*d.* about 180) and Tertullian (*d.* 220) are in substantial agreement.

The tendency of the doctrine concerning the Church at the close of the second century may be summed up in the words of *Hatch*: "The supremacy of the bishop and unity of doctrine were conceived as going hand in hand: the bishop was conceived as having what Irenæus calls the *charisma veritatis*; the bishop's seat was conceived as being, what St. Augustine later calls it, the *cathedra unitatis* and round the episcopal office revolved the whole vast system, not only of Christian administration and Christian organization, but also of Christian doctrine" (*Organ. of Early Christian Churches*, pp. 98, 99).

No exact definitions concerning the nature of the Church are found previous to the time of Cyprian. What the Early Fathers say concerning the nature of the Church is frequently so indefinite, that it is almost impossible fully to ascertain their real sentiments. But the inner and spiritual essence of the Church at this period was not altogether lost sight of. In their earlier writings both Irenæus and Tertullian emphasize the fact that the Church is heir of the truth and doctrine of the Apostles only in so far as she retains the presence and power of the Holy Spirit.

Cyprian, bishop of Carthage, almost lost sight of the inner or spiritual essence of the Church, and unduly emphasized the historical and visible existence of the Church. With him the unity of the Church is absolutely identified with that of the Episcopate. The bishop is the absolute vicegerent of Christ in things spiritual. Cyprian substitutes a *sacerdotal hierarchy of bishops* for the apostolic doctrine of the *universal priesthood* of all believers. He is the typical high-churchman of the Ante-Nicene age.

According to him the unity of the Church is secured 1) by a direct and unbroken succession of bishops from the time of the apostles, and 2) by the communication of special gifts of the Holy Ghost to all bishops at the time of ordination.

The bishops are the pillars and guardians of the unity of the Church. "There is one God, and Christ is one, and there is one Church, and one chair founded upon the rock by the word of the Lord" (*Ep.* 39, cap. 5) ... "This unity we ought firmly to hold and assert, especially those of us that are bishops who preside in the Church, that we may also prove the episcopate itself to be one and undivided... The episcopate is one, each part of which is held by each one for the whole" (*De unit. eccles.* cap. 5).

In a certain sense the bishops are the Church itself. No bishop, no church. "You ought to know that the bishop is in the Church, and the Church in the bishop; and if anyone be not with the bishop, that he is not in the Church." (*Ep.* 68 (66) 8). This is the famous formula of Cyprian's theory.

Holding that the Church was founded on St. Peter alone (as the Rock), he transferred the same superiority to the bishop of Rome as the successor of Peter, and thus traces to *the chair of St. Peter*, the source of the unity of the Church. "The chair of St. Peter is the principal Church whence sacerdotal unity is derived" (*Ep.* 54, cap. 14).

The bishop receives authority to teach and to exercise the power of the keys, as successors of the Apostles, by virtue of a vicarious ordination,—and not because called to the office by the whole Church. The bishop is appointed directly by God, is responsible directly to God, is inspired directly from God. See especially *Ep.* 68 (66).

In order to understand more clearly the development of the doctrine of the Church during the Ante-Nicene period, we may sum up, in this connection, some facts, which however will be more fully discussed where they properly belong.

The Greek word *ecclesia* literally means the body of those who are called out of the world to form an *ecclesia*, a church, an assembly, considered as a unity. There is this difference between the words *ecclesia* and *congregation* that the first regards believers as *separated* from the world, and the second regards them as *assembled* in one place, but the harmony of the two words lies in this, that men are called out of the world (*ecclesia*) that they may be assembled and united as saints in a *congregation*. The word *ecclesia* marks their relation to the world, the word *congregation* their relation to each other.

In Apostolic times, and for generations after, there was but one congregation in one city, however large that city might be. One congregational organization was retained even where the members were so numerous and so widely scattered as to require different places of worship and different pastors.

An essential part of the organization of the congregations was connected with the institution of the congregational pastorate, the office which was to superintend and spiritually rule the congregations, to conduct the public services, to administer the sacraments, to labor in the word and in doctrine, and to watch for souls, for the conversion of sinners and the building up of saints.

Various names and designations are given to pastors in the N.T. St. Paul gives us two lists, the first in 1 Cor. 12:28–30, and the second in Eph. 4:11, 12.

The N.T. title of the pastoral office, which covers teaching and preaching as well as oversight, is that of Presbyter or Elder, and Bishop. These two names are entirely co-ordinate. To these are committed the headships of congregations. A N.T. bishop is an elder or presbyter, and a N.T. presbyter or elder is a bishop.

The idea of a *ruling* eldership as of divine authority distinct from a pastorate, or the idea of a N.T. episcopate, is a pure misapprehension, without any warrant from Scripture and in absolute defiance of the history of the Church.

Jus divinum Presbyterianism involves the divine institution of lay elderships, and is even a more hopeless figment than *Jus divinum* diocesan Episcopacy. Neither view has any foundation in Scripture, nor in the history of the Church.

The supremest permanent office in the Christian congregation is that of the bishop-elder or pastor, one in kind, one in authority. The only other office of a permanent nature, of Apostolic appointment, in the congregation, is the *diaconate*. The pastorate (bishop-elder) and the diaconate were offices, not orders. The N.T. everywhere emphasizes the universal priesthood of all believers. (1 Pet. 2:5, 9.) At the close of the Apostolic age, the office of the presbyter-bishop, and the deacon was fully established, but as yet there was no trace of the diocesan Episcopate.

The words bishop and presbyter are synonymous in the Apostolic Age (Phil. 1:1; Acts 20:17, 28; 1 Pet. 5:1, 2; 1 Tim. 3:1, 8; Tit. 1:5, 7). Several bishops belonged to a single congregation. The time the first distinction arose between the terms elder and bishop was about 100 A. D. in the writings of Ignatius. He however does not know of the *diocesan* episcopate, but the bishop of whom he speaks is the pastor of a single congregation. "There is to every church one altar, and one bishop, with the presbytery and the deacons." All his references everywhere to a bishop are to the congregational episcopacy.

The congregational Episcopate developed out of the presbyterate. The title (bishop), common to all, came at length to be appropriated to the chief among them. Episcopacy was not a sudden creation. It arose from the demands of the times, and the needs of the churches,—the president of a body of presbyters being the direct occasion of the congregational episcopate.

History thus shows that by the middle of the second century each organized congregation had 1) its bishop; 2) its presbyters; and 3) its deacons. The transition was gradual. *a*) At first every congregation was distinct in its government,—congregations were not grouped by districts large or small, as later. *b*) Each congregation was governed by a body of elders or bishops perfectly coordinate, with not even a presiding head. This presbytery was a congregational one. *c*) The first step in the change was to give one of the bishop-presbyters a place as presiding bishop or presiding elder in the congregational presbytery. *d*) There was thus a gradual development of the office from the presbytery. *e*) From this point the Church in her liberty developed the diocesan Episcopacy. Three names are connected with this develepment, Ignatius, Irenæus, and Cyprian.

The Succession of Bishops at Rome.

The attempt to decipher the early history of Episcopacy at Rome is hopeless. *Schaff.* "The obscure chronology of the early bishops of Rome" is "veiled in impenetrable darkness." We have lists of Roman bishops (the catalogues of popes), but they are not to be relied on. What we positively know is that at the end of the first century the Roman Church was ruled by the mild presbyter-bishop Clemens, and at the close of the second century by the haughty Victor, the prototype of an Innocent or a Hildebrand.

Though it was a fundamental error to regard the Church as essentially an external organization (as Cyprian did), and though the distinction between the external marks of an outward institution and the internal marks which constitute the very essence of the Church, were lost sight of, nevertheless the inner and spiritual essence of the Church was still held by many. The Church was regarded after all as essentially *invisible*, and thus was not an object of *sight*, but became *an article of faith*.

This distinction between the *Visible* and *Invisible* Church, and the fact that the Church is essentially *invisible* is involved and implied in both the Apostles' Creed and the Nicene Creed. They do not say *I see*, but *I believe in* "the holy Christian Church"—*sanctam ecclesiam Catholicam* (Apostles' Creed), *I believe* "in one, holy, Christian, and Apostolic Church"—*eis mian hagian katholiken kai apostoliken ekklesian* (Nicene Creed).

In the Apostles' Creed the Church is regarded as a "holy Catholic Church," or universal Church, the Christian Church in its totality, *the communion of saints*, and this is linked with the words, "I believe in the Holy Ghost." This collocation implies that the Holy Ghost is the Father of this Church, and the expression "the communion of saints" reveals its internal character.

In the Niceno-Constantinopolitan Creed (381 A. D), the Church confesses that there is "one, Holy, Catholic, and Apostolic Church," and the collocation also indicates that the Church is the work of the Holy Ghost. This leads us to the *attributes* of the Church.

The Attributes of the Church as emphasized by the Church Fathers.

The *Unity* of the Church

The Church is "one." According to Scripture this *unity* consists in the fact that 1) all members of the Church are baptized by one baptism into one body and one Spirit (Eph. 4:4, 5); 2) all members are made partakers of one faith and one hope of their calling (Eph. 4:4, 5); 3) all have one Lord to whom they are united by one Spirit (Eph. 4:4, 5); 4) and all thus become one in their one God and Father (Eph. 4:6).

Five figures are used in Scripture to set forth the unity of the Church: 1) the *body* (1 Cor. 12:12–27); 2) the *vine* (John 15:1–9): 3) a *flock* (John 10:16); 4) a *kingdom* (Matt. 12:25); 5) a *temple* (Eph. 2:20–22).

This true idea of the unity of the Church was early perverted, and transferred to an external organized unity of the Church under the episcopate, though that episcopate was not yet diocesan. It was Cyprian, especially, as we have seen above, who unduly emphasized the historical and visible existence of the Church. Cyprian's doctrine of the Church identified the *invisible* Church with the *visible*, the *spiritual* unity of the Church with the external *unity of organization*, and in this lay its fallacy. With him the unity of the Church under the present order of things was no longer a matter of faith, but one of sight. Cyprian most fully develops his doctrine of the *unity, universality* and *exclusiveness* of the Church in his famous treatise *De Unitate Ecclesiæ*, written in the year 251. "He is not a Christian who is not in the Church of Christ." "No one can have God for his father who has not the Church for his mother." "Extra ecclesiam nulla salus."

With reference to the proposition "Outside of the Church there is no salvation," Marheineke truly says: "It is incorrect to say that this proposition was for the first time laid down by Augustine, in the fourth century, in the Donatist Controversy. It was only the necessary consequence and application of earlier principles, and was distinctly implied in the form which the doctrine of the Church had assumed since the time of Irenæus."

In opposition to heretics and to all who are not Christians, the Early Fathers uniformly asserted that "there is no salvation out of the Church." In the Apostolic Fathers Clemens Romanus, Ignatius and Hermes, this doctrine is identified with the doctrine of salvation in Christ alone, of which salvation the Church alone was the abode. It was believed and taught that within the visible, historical Church the work of the Holy Ghost for the salvation of men took place. This is emphasized in that famous expression of Irenæus: "Where the Church is, there is the Spirit of God; and where the Spirit of God is, there is the Church and all grace." Roman Catholicism, to this day, lays stress upon the first part of this proposition, and Protestantism on the second part.

Schaff: The Scriptural principle: "Out of *Christ* there is no salvation," was contracted and restricted to the Cyprianic principle: "Out of the (visible) *Church* there is no salvation"; and from this there was only one step to the fundamental error of Romanism: "Out of the *Roman* Church there is no salvation."

Cyprian's doctrine was subsequently developed, but broadened and deepened by *Augustine* in his conflict with Donatism. He held to a unity grounded and established in the Holy Ghost, but presenting itself to view in an external organism. With this view of Augustine was united the idea of a Church out of which there is no salvation. "They have not the love of God (toward them), who love not the unity of the Church, and for this reason it is seen that it is rightly said, the Holy Ghost cannot be received except in the Catholic Church." (De bapt. contra Donat. 3, 16.) This outward conception of the unity of the Church soon found a contradiction in the separation between the Oriental and Occidental Churches (692 A. D.).

The Holiness of the Church.

"I believe in one, *holy*, Catholic, and Apostolic Church."

The Church is *holy*, not because every one of the members of the visible Church is holy (for the visible Church is of a mixed character, *e. g.*, the Parable of the Tares, Matt. 12:24–30; the grain with the chaff, Matt. 3:12; the Parable of the Dragnet, Matt. 13:47–50; the sheep with the goats, Matt. 25:32, 33; the Parable of the Marriage Feast with guests bad and good, Matt. 22:10; the Vine with fruitful and unfruitful branches, John 15:2; the great house, with vessels, some unto honor, and some unto dishonor, 2 Tim. 2:20).

But 1) because the Church's Head, even Jesus Christ (Eph. 5:23), who rules (Heb. 3:6), nourishes and cherishes the Church (Eph. 5:29) is *holy* (Mark 1:24; Acts 3:14), and we are members of

His mystical body (Eph. 5:30); and 2) because the object of her foundation and her final aim is *holiness* (Eph. 5:27; Tit. 2:14).

3) All the Fathers emphasized the holiness of the Church. Origen ascribes it to "the Church in the proper sense." Augustine maintained that the Church consists of the sum total of all who are baptized, and that the (ideal) holiness of the Church was not impaired by the impure elements externally connected with it. He draws a distinction between "the true and the mixed body of the Lord" (De doct. Christ. 3, 32).

The Catholicity of the Church.

"I believe in one, holy, *Catholic*, and Apostolic Church."

The word *Catholic* is transferred and not translated from the Greek. It is found in Greek writers some centuries at least before the Christian era. It means *diffused throughout the whole, i.e., universal.* As used by the earliest Christian writers it denotes the "general" or "universal" Church in opposition to a particular body of Christians. In Luther's time the word *Catholic* had not been introduced into the German language. In the Apostles' Creed it is translated *Christliche*, in the Nicene Creed, *all-gemeine.* The best popular translation of *Catholic* (through the whole) is *Christian*, for the word *universal* falls short of its true meaning.

The phrase *Catholic Church* is first found in the writings of Ignatius. "Where Christ is, there is the Catholic Church" (Ign. ad Smyrn. 8), an affirmation closely corresponding with the Lutheran rendering "Christian Church." The word *Catholic* or universal, in its etymological sense *throughout the whole* involves universal extension in respect 1) to *place*, 2) to *time*, and 3) to *teaching.*

The Church Catholic in respect to Place or Extension. Our Lord bade His Apostles "Go into all the world, and preach the Gospel to the whole creation" (Mark 16:15). Athanasius: "It is Catholic because being poured forth it flows throughout the whole world" (De parab. Script. Qu. 37). Augustine: "It is called *Catholic* in Greek, because it is diffused throughout the whole world" (Epist. 53). So Cyril: "It is called catholic because it is throughout the world, from one end of it to the other" (Catech. 18, 23).

The Church Catholic in respect to Time. The Church is universal in respect to time, having endured throughout all ages, and is destined to endure until the end of time. This is fully stated by Augustine in various passages: The Church includes "the whole people of the saints from Abel to those who shall be born to the end of the world, and who shall believe on Christ" (In. Ps. 92); "all in heaven and all on earth" (Enchir. 56). All *space* and all *time* and eternity are covered by the conception of the word *Catholic.*

The Church Catholic in respect to Teaching. The Church is Catholic, not only in the sense that she is to embrace all mankind and all time, but she is commissioned to teach *universally the entire body of doctrines* which men ought to believe (Matt. 28:19, 20). Cyril: "It is called *Catholic* … because it teaches universally and completely one and all the doctrines which ought to come to men's knowledge concerning things both visible and invisible, heavenly and earthly; … and because it universally treats and heals the whole class of sins, which are committed by soul or body" (Catech. 18, 23).

In virtue of its catholicity (universality) in place, time, and teaching, the Church has a unity which excludes the continued existence of Judaism, or of any particular Church, denomination, or sect, which has risen in time and has fallen or may fall in time, and over against all particular churches, which are pure Churches, the Christian (Catholic or Universal) Church is a unity of the whole over against the parts.

Pure particular churches are but parts of the Church Catholic, and all particular pure churches together do not make up the Church Catholic, for its unity covers all time, all space, all number, what is past, what is, and what is to come—all earth and all heaven.

The Apostolicity of the Church.

"I believe in one, holy, Catholic, and *Apostolic* Church."

Though the exact word does not occur in the N.T., it is implied in Eph. 2:20 that the Church is Apostolic, for it is built upon the foundation laid by the Apostles and prophets.

The Church is apostolic also 1) because of her doctrinal and historical connection with the Apostles, 2) because she continually sets forth the doctrine of the Apostles, and remains steadfast therein, and 3) has entrusted to her the apostolic mission of preaching the Gospel to the whole world. This Apostolic character was constantly emphasized by the Fathers against the heretics, to confront and confute their innovations,—especially in the teaching of the Western Church.

We have already seen (61) what stress Irenæus lays upon "the apostolical tradition continuously preserved."

Tertullian (De Praescr. 20): "The Apostles founded churches in every city, from which all the other churches, one after another, derived the tradition of the faith and the seeds of doc trine, and are every day deriving them, that they may become Churches. Indeed, it is on this account only that they will be able to deem themselves apostolic, as being the offspring of apostolic Churches ... Therefore the churches, although they are so many and so great, comprise but the one primitive Church (founded) by the Apostles, from which they all (spring). In this way all are primitive, and all are Apostolic. Augustine especially develops this thought in his tract "On the Profit of Believing" (*De Utilitate Credendi*).

Over against the changes of opinions resting on insecure ground, the Fathers lay stress on the authority of the Church, which is claimed to be perpetuated from the Apostles, through the succession of Bishops or congregational pastors (see 61, 62 above.) Out of this train of thinking arose finally the claim of the Roman Primate as successor to the Apostolate of St. Peter. But such a conception of the Apostolicity of the Church has no warrant in Scripture, and is overthrown by the facts of Church History.

The Church can acknowledge no second hand apostolicity. At this hour the Church of Rome claims the control of the world on the basis of Apostolic tradition, and the Greek Church, supported by Apostolic tradition (and yet more to the purpose, by Apostolic writings), repudiates the claim of Rome with more than Protestant vehemence.

The Church of Jesus Christ is *Apostolic* because, and only as far as, it abides in the faith taught and in the sacraments administered and perpetuated by the Apostles, of which the only rule is the *Word* of which the Apostles are the preeminently inspired authors, and which they carried as the first great missionaries of the cross to all parts of the world.

Montanism, Novatianism, and *Donatism* arose in the effort by strict discipline to make the visible Church a holy Church. It was an attempt to whip the visible into the invisible Church:

1. Montanism, a movement which arose in Asia Minor (Phrygia) about 156–172 A. D., was a fanatical extreme of a laudable movement to lay more emphasis upon the discipline of the Church and upon the work of the Holy Spirit than the Church, amid the difficulties and temptations of the times, was doing. It had as its special task a reformation of Christian life, and Church discipline was regarded as highly necessary in view of the approaching Parousia and the setting up of the heavenly Jerusalem. Under the pretence of instituting a new and higher stage of revelation (by its doctrine of the Paraclete and their position that they were the privileged people of the Holy Ghost) they really undertook to correct the moral and religious doctrines of Christ and the Apostles as being defective and incomplete. They were most influential in North Africa, having greatly influenced Tertullian (*d.* 220), and Augustine (*d.* 430) speaks of the "Tertullianists" in his own time. They are regarded by the Ritschlian school of historical critics as the representatives of primitive, enthusiastic Christianity which had become "secularized" in the Catholic Church.

2. Although Montanism had been condemned, Novatian (Rome), after 251 A. D., became the leader of a party of *purists,* who taught that the Church has no right to give assurance of forgivenes to the fallen or such as have broken their baptismal vows by grievous sins (although they did not deny that God might forgive the sinner), and that the Church, being a communion of thoroughly pure members, should never endure any impure ones in its bosom, nor receive back any excommunicated ones, even after a full ecclesiastical course of penitence. Many of the old Montanists joined this movement, and the Novatians were still in existence in the sixth century.

3. The Donatists spread over all North Africa (311–415 A. D.), so named after Donatus the Great, elected Bishop of Carthage 313 A. D. They started from the principle that no one who has been excommunicated or deserves to be is fit for the performance of any sacramental action. With the Novatians they demanded the absolute purity of the Church, but admitted that by repentance Church fellowship could be regained. Augustine, about 400 A. D., began his unwearied attacks upon this sect.

In conflict with the Donatists Augustine was obliged to make distinctions which logically overthrew some of his earlier views of the organic exhibition of the unity of the Church. He drew a distinction between the members of the Church properly such, and not properly such. "There are some in the house of God after such a fashion as not to be themselves the very house of God" ... "Others are said to be in the house after such a sort, that they belong not to the substance of the house" (De Bapt. Contra Donat. 7, 51). He also distinguishes between the true Church and the mixed: "We ought to speak of the true and the mixed body of the Lord, or the true and the false, or some such name; because, not to speak of eternity, hypocrites cannot even now be said to be in Him, although they seem to be in His Church." ... "The Church declares itself to be at present both; and this because the good fish and the bad are for the time mixed up in one net" (De Doct. Chr. 3, 32).

In fact Augustine here draws that very distinction between the *essence* of the Church and what experience shows the visible Church actually to be, which was long after so forcibly emphasized in the Augsburg Confession and in the writings of the Reformers. But in spite of these juster views of Augustine and others of the same period, the tendency constantly increased to lay excessive stress upon the *external organism* of the Church, and to make Salvation dependent on loyalty, not to Christ, but to the Visible Church.

The Roman Catholic Church

This externalizing tendency came to its complete development in the Church of Rome. This Church identifies itself with the *invisible* Church, and regards its own hierarchical organism, with the Pope at its head as the bearer and organ of the Holy Ghost, who still supernaturally by His Inspiration acts upon the leaders of the Church, and that membership with it is the necessary condition of the salvation of every individual. Hence the Roman Catholic Church declares itself to be the alone saving and infallible Church.

A few citations will be sufficient to demonstrate what the Roman Church teaches on these points:

1. The first great factor in this development was Gregory VII (Hildebrand), unquestionably the greatest of all the Popes (1073–1085). He laid stress on the universal theocracy of the Church,

with the Pope, as vicar of Christ, at its head. He further maintained: "That the Roman Church never erred and never will err, as the Scriptures testify."

2. This theory of Hildebrand was upheld by Boniface VIII (1294–1303 A. D.) who definitely asserts: "we declare, affirm, and define, that subjection to the Roman Pontiff on the part of every creature is everywhere necessary for salvation." (Extrav. Comm. I, 8, 1.)

3. The Primacy of the Pope and his superior authority in relation to kings and princes was dogmatically set forth by Thomas Aquinas, the great Roman Catholic Dogmatician (*d.* 1274).

4. Perrone, the greatest Roman Catholic Dogmatician of this century (*d.* 1876) says (Vol. 1, §265): "Outside of the Catholic Church (Romish) there is no salvation."

5. Catechismus Romanus (I, 10, 18): "As this one Church cannot err in faith and in the discipline of morals, inasmuch as it is governed by the Holy Spirit, so all others which arrogate to themselves the name of the Church, inasmuch as they are led by the spirit of the devil, must of necessity be involved in the most pernicious errors of doctrine and morals." This means that as Rome is infallibly right everything outside of Rome is infallibly wrong.

6. Bellarmine (1542–1621), probably the greatest Apologist and controversialist of the Roman faith, in Antitheses to the Protestant doctrine of the Church, writes (De eccl. mil. 2): "Our judgment is that the one true Church is an assembly of men, bound together by the profession of the same Christian faith and in the communion of the same sacraments, under the government of lawful pastors and especially of the one vicar of Christ in the world. From which definition it may easily be gathered who belong to the Church and who do not belong to it. And this is the difference between our judgment and all others, that all others require internal virtues to constitute any one a part of the Church and moreover represent the true Church as invisible; but we believe that all virtues are found in the Church, yet we do not think that in order that a man may in some sense be said to be a part of the true Church, internal virtue is requisite, but only external profession of faith and communion of the sacraments.

For the Church is an assembly of men just as visible and palpable as the Kingdom of France or the Republic of Venice."

7. Pope Leo XIII (1878–1903), in his Encyclical Letter *Satis cognitum* also maintains that the unity of the Church requires a supreme authority, and that a supreme authority necessitates an earthly head. "Since Christ willed that His kingdom should be visible, He was obliged, when He ascended into heaven, to designate a vicegerent on earth." ... "Jesus Christ, therefore, appointed Peter to be the head of the Church; and He also determined that the authority instituted in perpetuity for the salvation of all should be inherited by his successors, in whom the same permanent authority of Peter himself should continue."

In a summary, according to the Roman theory, the Roman Catholic Church has *four characteristics*, and *four marks or notes*. The four *characteristics* are:

1) The Roman Church is a *neccessary* institution, for outside of it there is no salvation.

2) She is *indefectible*, that is to say, she will never fail nor pass away, because she is divine.

3) She is *infallible*, and cannot err, because the Holy Spirit preserves both the *Teaching* Church (*ecclesia docens*) and the *Believing* Church (*ecclesia credens*, the people whose duty it is to believe what they are taught by their pastors) free from error in faith and morals.

4) She is *visible*, and the Pope of Rome is the Vicar of Christ, appointed by Him as the Head of the Church on earth.

The four *marks*, according to the Roman theory, are:

1) *Unity.* This unity is one of faith, of discipline, of worship, of morals, etc., under one visible Head, the Pope of Rome.

2) *Holiness.* The Roman theory ascribes holiness to the Church as a corporation, "because she is consecrated and dedicated to God," and asserts that she alone teaches holy doctrine, and "to possess true holiness, we must belong to this Church," and that within her communion are holy people.

3) *Catholic.* "Universal spreading in its jurisdiction throughout all nations"; "because all who desire eternal salvation must cling to and embrace her, like those who entered the ark, to escape perishing in the flood" (Rom. Cat.); *Catholic*, because she teaches *quod ubique, quod semper, quod ab omnibus creditum est*, "what is everywhere, always, and by all believed."

4) *Apostolicity.* Apostolic, because founded by the Apostles, possessing an unbroken succession of pastors from Apostolic times, rightfully ordained, lawfully sent, and teaching Apostolic doctrine. "The Holy Ghost, who presides over the Church, governs her by no other than Apostolic men, and this Spirit, first imparted to the Apostles, has, by the infinite goodness of God, always continued in the Church" (Rom. Cat.).

Bellarmine in his enthusiasm increased the number of the *marks* or *notes* of the Church to *fifteen*: 1) The name Catholic, 2) antiquity, 3) abiding duration, 4) amplitude, or multitude and variety of believers, 5) succession of bishops from the Apostles, 6) agreement in doctrine with the ancient Church, 7) union of members among themselves and with the Head, the Pope of Rome, 8) sanctity of doctrine, 9) efficacy of doctrine, 10) sanctity in life presented in the Fathers, 11) glory of miracles, 12) light of prophecy, 13) confession of adversaries, 14) unhappy end of her enemies, and 15) temporal felicity conferred upon those who defend her.

The Romish Doctrine of the Supremacy of the Pope.

The Roman Catholic theologians have defended this view on two great grounds, 1) on the ground of *reason*, and 2) on the ground of *authority*.

On the ground of *reason* they maintain that the visible body of the Church must have a visible head, that the Church on earth, consisting of men, must have a human head, and that unity ceases to be possible unless there is an earthly center of unity.

We answer: This unity under one visible head is not of necessity, 1) because the Church could as well be governed by an aristocracy, by many bishops equal among themselves, as by a monarchy, the Pope; 2) because the visible Church on earth, after all, is only a part of the Church, for the Church includes the departed saints and many yet unborn. We grant that the Church as a body must have a head, but it is not required by logic that a part of a body must have a head, and the Head of the whole body of the Church is our Lord Jesus Christ, who as the God-Man, by virtue of His true humanity, has been exalted on high to be Head over all things to the Church, visible and invisible. We grant that earthly unity is desirable, but this is not in any way a true mark of the Church, for true unity is mainly invisible, and consists in union one with another in the true Head of the Church, Jesus Christ, by a living faith.

On the ground of *authority* the Roman Church has urged that the Pope is the visible Head of the Church, and to be apart from the Pope is to be severed from the Church. This must be inviolably maintained for these reasons:

1) This was Christ's will, as He appointed Peter *alone* to be the founder of Christianity, and the visible Head of the whole Church Militant, the *Rock* on which the Church was built;

2) To Peter was granted the primacy of power and jurisdiction over the Church Catholic, as well as infallibility for defining doctrine concerning faith or morals;

3) This supremacy and infallibility were both transmitted to his perpetual successors in the See of Rome, and the Roman Pontiff is the successor of Peter.

This is the traditional doctrine, and the practice of the Roman Church.

We answer in the first place: The Supremacy of St. Peter in the Roman Catholic sense is *pure fiction*, and there is no evidence for it whatever in Scripture, or in the unanimous con sent of the Fathers. Scripture gives us no evidence whatever that Peter *alone* was appointed to be the founder of Christianity, and the Head of the Church.

The proof of the Roman theory, that Christ constituted the Apostle Peter universal head of the Church and conceded to him a primacy of power and jurisdiction over the Church, is not found in the three passages cited from the Gospels (Matt. 16:17–19; Luke 22:31, 32; John 21:15–17), known as the *Petrine texts*.

Taking up, first, the passage John 21:15–17, we may remark that the Roman Church maintains that here we have a record of the gift to St. Peter of jurisdiction over all the people of Christ. They find it in "Feed my sheep" (John 21:17). They base their whole doctrine of *Jurisdiction* over the Apostles and the whole Church on such a slender foundation, forgetting that Peter with the Apostles are also spoken of as sheep (Matt. 10:16), and that all pastors equally have this same office of "feeding the Church of God" (Acts 20:28), and that Peter himself exhorts his "fellow-elders" to feed the flock of God (1 Pet. 5:2). Peter did not at this time, nor at any other, receive "the privilege of jurisdiction" over the Church, nor over John —witness the saying of Christ, in this very connection, to Peter —"What is that to thee? Follow thou Me" (John 21:22). This whole passage has its great significance in this, that St. Peter is here re-instated after his denial of Christ.

On Luke 22:31, 32 they base their doctrine that Peter was granted infallibility, and charged with guiding the faith of the Apostles —"When once thou hast turned again, establish thy brethren." Here Peter's fall is foretold and Christ encourages him, that after his repentance he should build up the rest that they sin not as he has done. To strengthen others by confession of one's weakness and sin, and to encourage others, does not bestow *infallibility* nor give primacy and authority over others.

We come now to the last, and only important passage, on which Rome lays stress, Matt. 16:18, "Thou art *Petros*, and upon this *petra* I will build my Church; and the gates of Hades shall not prevail against it." Rome teaches that from this verse we learn that Peter is the *rock* in his own person, and that the primacy is here conferred on him. Of this doctrine of the Church of Rome Plumptre very forcibly remarks: "The interpretation which has assumed *a*) that the promise made the Apostle himself the *rock* on which the Church itself was built, *b*) that it conveyed to him a permanent supremacy and infallible authority, *c*) that the supremacy and infallibility were both transmitted by him to his successors, *d*) that those successors are to be found in the Bishops of Rome and in them only,—hardly deserves a notice, except as an instance of a fantastic development worthy of the foremost place in any exhibition of the monstrosities of exegesis." *Comm. on 1 Peter*, p. 14.)

We hold that the Roman theory cannot be deduced from their main passage, Matt. 16:18, for these general reasons:

1) Christ gave a like calling to all the Apostles (Matt. 28:18–20).

2) The power given to Peter in Matt. 16:18, 19, as to the power of the keys (loosing and binding) is given in Matt. 18:18 and John 20:21–23, to all Apostles, and to the Church in general.

3) The very opposite is specifically taught in Eph. 2:20, for the Church "is built upon the foundation of the apostles and prophets, Christ Jesus himself being the chief corner stone," and not on Peter as a person.

4) The whole history of the Early Church as recorded in the Acts and in the Epistles of Paul and Peter is opposed to such a view.

a) No one disputes the fact that Peter was the recognized leader of the Apostles, and this is plainly seen in the first twelve chapters of Acts. Of the *ten* occasions in which he assumes the leadership, *five* are especially prominent: 1) He proposes the election of an apostle (Acts 1:15, 21, 22); 2) He preaches the first great Missionary Sermon (Acts 2:14–40); 3) He passes judgment on Ananias and Sapphira (Acts 5:3–11); 4) He preaches the first Missionary Sermon to the Gentiles (10:34–48); 5) St. Paul after his return from Arabia, goes up to Jerusalem to consult with Peter (Gal. 1:18).

5) But not one of these acts singly, nor all of them collectively, give any proof that Peter was the Head of the Church, and had the primacy of Jurisdiction and of authority. In fact the narrative of the election of Matthias (Acts 1:21–26) furnishes evidence against it,—for according to the Roman theory Peter should have filled the vacant place of Judas on his own authority. So also the case of Ananias and Sapphira is a miraculous judgment, in a special case, not in any way different in kind or degree from that exercised repeatedly by St. Paul (Acts 13:6–12; 1 Tim. 1:20; 1 Cor. 5:3).

6) There are three facts recorded in the Acts which plainly show that Peter did not have the supremacy as maintained by the Roman Church. 1) Peter was one of those sent by the Apostles to Samaria (Acts 8:14–17). According to the Roman Church Peter ought to have been the sender and not the one sent. 2) Peter was called to defend his conduct in the matter of Cornelius by the other Apostles and the brethren at Jerusalem (Acts 11:1–4). 3) In the council of Jerusalem the chief place was occupied by James, who pronounced the decision of the Council (Acts 15:13–22). Peter has here no more prominence than Barnabas or Paul.

7) Peter himself nowhere claims such supreme personal authority, as ruler or Head of the Church. Three passages may be quoted, Acts 10:25, 26; 1 Pet. 5:1, "I exhort, who am a fellow-elder, and a witness of the sufferings of Christ;" 2 Pet. 3:1, 2, "through your Apostles."

8) So likewise St. Paul knows of no such supremacy, nor does he anywhere recognize it, for he reckons himself "not a whit behind the very chiefest Apostles" (2 Cor. 11:5). 1) His Apostolate and his teaching is entirely independent of Peter (Gal. 1:1; 2:11, 12); 2) He claims to be the Apostle of the Gentiles (Rom. 11:3), independent of Peter, not building upon another man's foundation (Rom. 15:15–20); 3) Peter, in Paul's view, had no part in the founding of the Church at Rome, nor any claim upon it, either previous or co-existing (Rom. 15:15–20); 4) Paul explicitly declares that the care of all the churches is his daily task (2 Cor. 11:28), and he ordains rules to be observed in all the churches (1 Cor. 7:17; 11:1, 2).

9) Among these general reasons we may also refer to various facts in Peter's personal life opposed to the Roman theory: 1) Peter is the only Apostle sternly rebuked by Christ (Matt. 16:23); 2) He is the only one of the Apostles, except Judas Iscariot, who denied Christ with an oath (Matt. 26:69–75); 3) He is the only Apostle of whom it is said that he erred on a point of doctrine and morals (Gal. 2:6–14); 4) in the history of the Church of the N.T. he was entirely overshadowed by Paul; 5) we have no evidence in Scripture that Peter had anything to do with the Church at Rome.

10) Such a view can never be proven, either exegetically or historically.

We hold that the word *rock* in Matt. 16:18 does not refer to Peter as a person in the sense that the Romanist claims, implying that Peter was invested with a permanent primacy capable of being transmitted to his successor.

1) To prove this Rome must show that Peter *alone* was the founder of Christianity. Scripture teaches just the reverse, as has already been shown (77, 1, 2).

2) Rome must prove that Peter was the vicegerent of God and the Sovereign of the whole Christian Church. There is no evidence for this in this passage, and the whole teaching of the N.T. is against it, nor can it be shown by any proof historical or otherwise.

3) Rome must show that this supposed primacy and authority was transmissible, of which there is no evidence in Scripture or in history.

4) Rome must show that Peter lived and died at Rome, which is probably true but not certain, and that he was, rather than Paul, the head of the Church at Rome, of which there is no evidence at all.

5) Rome must show that Peter's supposed transmissible authority was actually transmitted to the leading official of the Church at Rome. Of this there is no evidence in Scripture or in history, nothing but a comparatively late tradition. The early history of the Christian Church shows indeed that the Church at Rome, as the church of the Imperial City, had a great natural prominence, but it equally gives evidence that this prominence was not supreme, or had any sovereignty, recognized or claimed. (After *Broadus.*)

In addition to the later Roman interpretation of the word *rock*, three other interpretations have been given.

1) Some regard the *rock, Christ* Himself (so finally Augustine, Chemnitz, Calovius, and in modern times Wordsworth and James Morison). This interpretation expresses indeed a great truth, for Christ is the true Rock, the one and only foundation of the Church, and "other foundation can no man lay than that which is laid, which is Jesus Christ" (1 Cor. 3:11), and no one lays greater stress upon this than Peter himself (1 Pet. 2:6–8), but certainly such an interpretation does not give the simple and primary meaning of our Savior's words.

2) Others maintain that the *rock* is *the faith and confession of Peter* (so already the great majority of the Early Fathers, among whom may be mentioned Gregory of Nyssa, Cyril of Alexandria, Chrysostom, Theophylact, Hilary, Ambrose, Augustine, and most Protestants since the Lutheran Reformation). This interpretation also brings to light a great and glorious truth, that the Church of God is built upon the doctrine preached by the Apostles and Prophets, but surely this is not an exact interpretation of what Christ says, for "the Church is not built upon abstract doctrines and confessions, but upon living persons believing and confessing the truth (Eph. 2:20; 1 Pet. 2:4–6; Gal. 2:9; Rev. 21:14)."

3) The third view, and the most natural interpretation, which has the best exegetical foundation, refers the passage indeed to Peter—that he is the rock—not however in his own person as such, nor in his office, but as the representative of the Apostles, as professing in their name the true faith, and as such is entrusted

with laying the foundation of the Church as the first preacher and witness to both Jews and Gentiles (Acts 2 and 10). So already among others Bengel (on Matt. 16:18): "Unquestionably the Church is built upon the Apostles (Eph. 2:20; Rev. 21:14), inasmuch as they were both the first to believe themselves, and the means of leading others to believe. And herein Peter exercised a certain prerogative as chief, without any prejudice to the equality of power in all the Apostles; for he was both the first to gain over many Jews (Acts 2), and the first to admit the Gentiles to Gospel privileges (Acts 10). Besides the commands, 'establish thy brethren' (Luke 17:32) and 'Feed my lambs', 'Feed my sheep' (John 21:15, 17) were specially given to him. And there is great significance in the fact, that the glorious name *Rock* (elsewhere generally assigned to Christ Himself, 1 Cor. 10:4, etc.) is here attributed to Peter, who is always first named, and placed in the foremost rank in the lists of the Apostles (Matt. 10:2). And all this may be safely affirmed; *for what has this to do with Rome.*" And Meyer adds: "This primacy must be impartially conceded, though without involving those inferences which Romanists have founded upon it; for Peter's successors are not for a moment thought of by Jesus, neither can the Popes claim to be his successors, nor was Peter himself ever bishop of Rome, nor had he any more to do with the founding of the Church at Rome than the Apostle Paul."

This can be the only true interpretation of this passage. It has well been said, that no other explanation would probably at the present day be offered by Protestant commentators, but for the fact that the obvious meaning has been so abused by the Roman Church to the support of their theory. This interpretation can be maintained without periling, in the least degree, any of the great principles of Protestantism. This view has been accepted by many of the greatest modern exegetes (Huther, Meyer, Weiss, Alford, Geikie, Farrar, Schaff, Gloag, Broadus, and others).

As a proof that the Roman Church cannot even rely for their interpretation of Matt. 16:18, with reference to the primacy and "privilege" of Peter, on "the *unanimous* consent of the fathers" it will be sufficient to refer to the famous speech of Archbishop Kenrick of St. Louis in the Vatican Council (*printed* but not *delivered*), Naples, 1870 (edited by Dr. Bacon, printed by American Tract Society). As a member of the Council he, with many others, was opposed to the doctrine of the Infallibility of the Pope, and to support his position he quotes a pamphlet (the scholarship of which we can accept) showing that among the Early Fathers the following interpretations were held as to the meaning of the word *rock*: 1) That the word refers to *Peter*, accepted by *seventeen* fathers—among them Origen, Cyprian, Jerome, Hilary, Cyril of Alexandria, Leo the Great, Augustine; 2) *all* the Apostles, whom Peter represented by virtue of the primacy; taught by *eight* fathers—among them Origen, Cyprian, Jerome, Augustine, Theodoret; 3) the *faith* which Peter had professed. This interpretation is regarded as the weightiest of all, since it is followed by *forty-four* fathers and doctors; 4) that the word *rock* refers to *Christ*; followed by *sixteen* doctors.

The reason some of the Fathers are cited in holding two or more views is because they take it in different senses, at different times, and sometimes combine two views, sometimes leaning to one or the other side (see citations in Littledale, *The Petrine Claims*, pp. 74–79).

We can thus fairly conclude that the Roman theory of Peter's primacy and jurisdiction has no foundation whatever in Scripture nor in early tradition, and is altogether pure fiction. There is no basis whatever, either Scriptural or historical, for the huge fabric of Papal claims.

We answer, in the second place: The Pope of Rome is neither successor to Peter in the Episcopal chair, nor head nor monarch of the Christian Church.

History knows nothing of an episcopate of Peter at Rome. Some writers of great learning (like De Wette, Baur, Hase, Holtz-mann, Lipsius, Winer, etc.) deny that Peter was ever at Rome, but the fact of Peter's residence at Rome after 64 A. D. is accepted (on the testimony of the Early Fathers) by most modern scholars. But "the Roman tradition of a twenty or twenty-five years' episcopate of Peter in Rome is unquestionably a colossal chronological mistake" (Schaff).

Littledale (*The Petrine Claims*) cites all the extant evidence to be found in the Ante-Nicene period (*nineteen* passages), and sums up his investigation in these words: "No tittle of proof is derivable from the fairly copious remains of the ecclesiastical literature of the first three centuries, that St. Peter was ever Bishop of Rome, or that he transmitted the peculiar privilege of supremacy and infallibility to his successors in the See" (p. 180).

The real basis of the ultramontane claim of Rome is Jerome's Latin version of the *Chronicle* of Eusebius, where, under the year 40, we read: "Peter the Apostle, after he had first founded the Church at Antioch, is sent to Rome, and preaching the Gospel there, he abode as bishop for twenty-five years." But owing 1) to discrepancies between the Armenian, Syrian, and Latin Versions, 2) to the temptation of copyists continually to alter by adding matter to bring the annals down to date, and 3) to the entire silence on these points at issue in the more detailed history of this period as given in the famous *History* by the same writer, we cannot in any way rely on this testimony, for it evidently is an interpolation by some unknown scribe, at some earlier date.

It is not till the Post-Nicene period, at the close of the fourth century, that the episcopate of St. Peter at Rome is clearly alleged as a matter of fact, and the writer (Optatus of Milevis, *d.* after 386) knows more about the details and is more positive about them than any writer of the first three centuries. But Epiphanius (*d.* 403) in opposition to Optatus, expressly says that we have no accurate knowledge about this topic, since there is conflicting documentary evidence. (See Littledale, *The Petrine Claims.*)

There is therefore no historical basis whatever to prove that Peter was ever Bishop at Rome. If Peter was an Apostle, he could not have been a Bishop. A New Testament bishop was the pastor of a congregation. When in the second century diocesan bishops arose, they were the heads of a limited province. Peter was not the pastor of a congregation, nor the head of a diocese. If Peter had been a bishop of Rome, the present bishops of Rome are not his successors —not in doctrine, for their teachings are in conflict with his teachings, nor in life.

Even were it granted that Peter had a supremacy among the Apostles, that would not prove that his supremacy was capable of transmission to any one, or that if it could be transmitted, it would of a necessity be transferred to the future bishops of a locality in which Peter had lived, or that the place where he last labored would be the one in which the transmission would be kept up, over against the other places in which he also had labored.

As regards the second point, the Church knew nothing before Constantine's time of a visible head, and after the rise of the claims of the Bishops of Rome, an immense part of Christen dom, embracing the most venerable and august sees, ignored those claims and continued to be governed by Patriarchs and in other ways.

1) The Greek Church, the most ancient part of Christendom, is as strongly opposed to the claims of the Papacy as Protestantism, and is more intensely bitter.

2) The special dignity of the Popes is altogether a matter of purely human origin and arrangement.

3) The earliest concessions, looking to any primacy, made to the Bishop of Rome, conceded simply a primacy of honor, because of the political importance of the city, Rome.

4) The primacy of power and Jurisdiction was expressly denied to the Pope in Canon 28 of the Council of Chalcedon, 451, A. D. "We, following in all things the decisions of the holy fathers, ... do also determine and decree the same things respecting the privileges of the most holy city of Constantinople, the new Rome. For the fathers properly gave the primacy to the throne of the elder Rome, *because this was the imperial city.*"

5) When the Roman legates at this Council (Chalcedon, 451 A. D.) produced a forged copy of the Nicene Canons, containing, in the Sixth Canon, the words "*The Roman See has always had the Primacy,*" the Judges, after hearing the whole case, ruled that the alleged canon was unauthentic and an interpolation.

We have also seen that the claim of Rome cannot be based upon Patristic testimony, and is absolutely contrary to the facts in the case. We can fitly close this discussion on the *Supremacy of the Pope* in the words of a Roman Catholic writer and Professor, written when opposing the decrees of the Vatican Council (to which however he submitted before his death): "In the history of the human mind, there is no question, theological, philanthropical, historical, or otherwise, which has been so disgraced by falsehood, bad faith, and the whole work of the forgers, *as Papal Authority.* I repeat it, *It is a question utterly gangrened by fraud.*"

Papal Infallibility has not a single proof in its favor either in Scripture or in history. It is the doctrine of the Church of Rome that the *ex cathedra* decisions of the Pope, in matters of faith and morals, are infallible. The entire claim of Papal Infallibility rests on the Roman view of the Supremacy of Peter, and on their theory that the Pope has fallen heir to all Peter's privileges, a theory, as we have already seen, utterly without any foundation in Scripture or in history.

The Vatican Council affirmed the Papal Infallibility in 1870 on the basis of the three "Petrine texts," by a method of interpretation which cannot be maintained.

The Bishop of Rome was not regarded in the Early Church as an infallible teacher and ruler.

Pope Liberius in 357 A. D. subscribed an Arian creed, and anathematized St. Athanasius as a heretic. At the sixth General Council at Constantinople (681 A. D.), Pope Honorius was universally condemned as a heretic, for being a Monothelite, and every Pope for several centuries had to renew the anathema, at the time of his coronation.

The Western Church (on the principle that Popes may err in the discharge of their office, and that they are subject to the discipline of the collective Church), on its own authority has deposed Popes John XII., Benedict IX., Gregory VI., Gregory XII., and John XXIII.—the last in express terms as "simoniac, sorcerer, schismatic, and heretic."

To prove that Rome may err, and that she does not always teach the same, we need only refer to the famous work (*Sic et Non*) of Abelard (*d.* 1142), or give one illustration. Pius IX. on Dec. 8th, 1854, decreed the doctrine of the Immaculate Conception of the Blessed Virgin Mary —a tenet which had been denied, and regarded as heresy, by orthodox Catholics, including *fourteen* Popes, for a thousand years,—a doctrine which is contrary to the well-nigh "unanimous teaching of the Fathers."

Such was the terrible condition of the Roman Church during the tenth century, that a Roman Catholic Archbishop, writing at the close of the sixteenth century, says of this period: "This period was unfortunate in so far that during nearly 150 years about *fifty Popes* have fallen away from the virtues of their predecessors, being *apostates* or *apostatical*, rather than *apostolical.*" Nothing further need be said to prove the falsity of their theory.

Though the Roman Church claims infallibility, no Roman Catholic until within our own day has been able, from any utterance of the Church, to say where this infallibility lies.

1) Some said it lies in the Pope (ultramontanism);

2) Others said that it lies in a General Council (Gallicanism);

3) Still others that it lies in the concurrent action of the General Council and the Pope.

4) Even the Council of Trent, whose silence in general about the doctrine concerning the Church is very striking, did not decide the question.

5) After the lapse of centuries the Vatican Council of 1870 decided this question.

6) The matter was so adroitly arranged, that a Council, acknowledged by the Romanists to be General, with the Pope at its head, declared *that the infallibility lies in the Pope.* No matter what view any one may have had before, he must now admit that it lies in the Pope. *a*) If he said so before, his opinion is confirmed; *b*) If he said, Infallibility lies in a General Council, that General Council has declared that it lies in the Pope; *c*) If he ascribe it to both, both have said, it belongs to the Pope.

With the fall of the doctrines of the *Supremacy* and the *Infallibility* of the Pope, also falls to the ground the Roman doctrine of the *continued Inspiration* of the leaders of the Church, for Rome without any foundation in Scripture or history, holds to a living apostolate in the Church, perpetuating itself through all time, an inspiration constantly kept up in the representatives of the Church.

With reference to the other characteristics and marks of the Church emphasized by the Romanists, we may reply:

1. Some of these marks are entirely fallacious, being in no respect essential marks of the Church.

2. So far as these marks imply pure doctrine and the administration of the right sacraments, the notes are indeed correct, but they apply either very imperfectly or not at all to the Church of Rome.

3. The statement of the marks or notes of the Church is based upon the presumption that the Church of Rome is the only true and universal Church, and the definition is made to suit to that which her admirers suppose her to be. They do not test her by a true definition, but they test the definition by her.

We may answer the different points emphasized by Bellarmine (74, 11) in the following way (covering the whole position of the Romanists):

The name Catholic. The Catholic name may be without the true Catholic or Christian faith, as it was among the Novatians and Donatists, who claimed by pre-eminence and to the exclusion of all others, to be the true Catholics, and the faith may be without the name. The name is ecclesiastical, not divine, and the thing which is divine may be expressed by other names.

The Church may be called Catholic with respect to *quality* or with respect to *quantity.* The Roman Church is not *Catholic* with respect to *quality*, i.e., in her doctrine and faith, nor does she profess the faith which the whole body of believers has always professed. She is not the true and Christian Church, as tested by Scripture and the teaching of the Early Church. Nor is the Roman Church *Catholic* with respect to *quantity*, for she has only a few million more adherents than are arrayed against her in the Greek and Oriental Churches and the Protestant Churches, all of which deny her arrogant pretensions.

Antiquity. But error may also be old. Tertullian well says, Without the Word of God, antiquity is of no value. Truth is older than all.

Abiding duration. But error and evil have also pertinacity of life. The empire of falsehood has stood for ages and still stands apparently unshaken. Both truth and error will stand until the harvest.

Multitude of believers. But the world is wider and contains more adherents than the Church. Even among professed Christians the Roman Catholic Church has barely a majority.

Succession of bishops from the Apostles. The falsity of the theory underlying this statement has already been shown. We have no warrant in Scripture or in history that any authority or Jurisdiction in the special Roman sense belonged to Peter, or that this "Privilege of Peter" was transferred to the bishops of Rome. The canonical succession of the Roman Catholic bishops is in many respects more than doubtful, but even if the theory were sound and the canonical succession ascertainable in the Church of Rome, the Greek Church, and the whole body of Oriental Sects (like the Nestorians), and the Church of England, and the

Lutheran Church of Sweden and Norway, have the same sort of succession, and all these deny the position taken by Rome.

Apostolicity, or agreement in doctrine with the Ancient Church. But the Roman Church, in many points, is not in unison with the doctrine of the Ancient Church, nor with the Apostolic doctrine. The teaching of the Roman Church – "Outside of the visible Church, that is, the Roman Catholic Church, there is no salvation"—is false and contrary to Scripture. It is only of the *invisible* Church that the proposition holds good: "Outside of the Church is no salvation." This is but another way of saying— "without faith in Jesus Christ it is impossible to be saved."

a) Within the visible Church there has been and always will be an invisible Church holding to the truth as it is in Jesus, and holding to Jesus through the truth, and outside of this invisible Church there is no revealed possibility of salvation.

b) The saved are not to be found in the world, but in the visible Church; and in the visible Church they are to be found not among those who are simply *in* but not *of* it, but among its true members, living believers and saints.

c) Romanism is arrayed against the genuine teaching of the Early Church, as well as against the genuine Apostolic doctrine as recorded in Scripture.

External unity with the Pope of Rome. But salvation does not depend upon an external unity with the visible Church under the Jurisdiction of a Pope. See 78. The true unity of believers is a communion of saints one with another in the true head of the Church, in Jesus Christ, which is brought about by a living faith in Christ. Nor can even this external unity be found in the Church of Rome.

It has well been said, "There is actually no Church in the whole world which has been so conspicuously, so frequently, and so fatally divided and rent by schisms." There have been no fewer than *thirty-nine* Anti-popes, and the one who was in each case ultimately recognized was the one who had stronger friends, larger armies, or a longer purse, than the unsuccessful claimant.

The Great Schism lasted from 1378 to 1417, and rival lines of Pontiffs were kept up, and no one can say now which claimant at any time was the true Pope.

The Jealousies of the rival religious Orders (Franciscans versus Dominicans, Jesuits versus other Orders) answer precisely to the sects of Protestantism, in their origin, rise, decay, and denominational rivalry.

Sanctity of Doctrine. The doctrine of the Church of Rome is in many respects in conflict with holiness, and as compared with the pure Gospel has shown itself inoperative in the lives of men. Some of Rome's greatest teachers, like Pascal, have shown that the ruling construction of morals in the Church of Rome is full of abominations. Estimates have been made in Protestant countries, showing that the Roman Catholic Church contributes, on an average, from eight to ten times her share of criminals to our prisons.

Efficacy of doctrine. An examination of the manuals of the Confessional and the Roman works on Casuistry (like Liguori's *Moral Theology*; Gury's *Comp. Theol. Moral.*) show that the Church of Rome is full of corrupting tendencies. In fact Liguorianism is fatal to holiness of teaching. Liguori (1732–1787) revived Probabilism, which is now the ordinary rule of confessors in the Roman Church, the doctrine, that in matters of conscience, "of two opinions it is lawful to follow the *less probable*, provided that the opinion rests on solid grounds" (*Gury*). Not only is the tendency of these text-books immoral, but utterly subversive of what is ethically right—e.g., a man may swear aloud to any false statement, provided he add some true circumstances in an undertone, unheard by the bystanders; or a man may purjure himself before a Judge, if any loss or inconvenience would follow to a witness from speaking the truth; etc.

Sanctity in life presented in the Fathers. There have been and are many earnest and devout souls within the Roman Church. But many of those enrolled as Saints have not a clear title, especially among the Popes. The Romàn Church too often has departed from the spirit of the early saints and from their sanctity, as she has from their doctrine. It has been truly said, that of all Churches ever professing the Christian faith, "*Rome has sunk lowest, longest, and oftenest;* she has been the foulest cesspool of wickedness, profligacy, "depravity of all kinds; she has had the greatest number of abandoned criminals among her Bishops." *One-fifth* of all the Popes who have ever sat in Rome have been charged with *grevious criminality.*

Glory to miracles. Her claims to miracles are barefaced impositions.

Light of Prophecy. A claim without any foundation.

Confession of adversaries. The testimony is directly the opposite.

Unhappy end of her enemies. Only, however, if. brought about by Rome herself. She kills her enemies and then appeals to her murders as a divine vindication of her purity. Her bloody persecutions have exhausted all the powers of diabolical ingenuity in torturing and killing the saints of the Lord Most High.

Temporal felicity conferred upon those who defend her. It is just the reverse. The men and nations who have done most for her overthrow, have been distinguished by a peculiar blessing of God. Contrast Italy, Spain, and South America, with Germany, England and the United States.

The Protestant Church (Based upen *Krauth*)

The weak point of Protestantism lies in its division into so many denominations and sects over against the compactness and seeming unity of Rome. The attempt to excuse the divisions by asserting that unity of doctrine is not necessary, and that diverse doctrines and heresy are of little importance, only aggravates the evil.

The Reformation originally was apparently a unit in doctrine. Luther and Melanchthon, Zwingli and Calvin, whose names are now divided between two great generic tendencies of Evangelical Protestantism, were in general alike in the faith in their earliest reformatory movements. They divided not on the *principle* which made them Reformers, but on the *results.*

As Protestantism grounded itself on the *formal* principle, that Scripture alone is the only rule of faith, and as Protestantism was almost at once divided into two sections differing widely on some points of doctrine, both sides appealing with the same confidence to Scripture, Rome instantly availed herself of this, and maintained that the error of Protestantism lay in its claim to the right of *private judgment* in the interpretation of Scripture.

The inference was irresistible, either the Scripture is not the only rule of faith (as the Romanists hold, and therefore lay most stress on *tradition*), or one, or other, or both Protestant parties (Lutheran and Reformed) misapplied the rule or principle.

Protestantism must seek the real cause of its tendency to division. The cause of Protestant divisions lies in general in the limitation, ignorance, narrowness, and passions of men. But men are equally limited, narrow, and hasty in the Church of Rome, so the real cause must lie elsewhere. It must lie in some shape, either in the abuse, or in the imperfect application, of private judgment in the interpretation Scripture. The Lutheran and Reformed Theologians had different views as to how the principle should be applied, which they acknowledged in common.

There was a difference as to the way in which they regarded *the silence* of Scripture. Both sides agreed that if a certain sense of Scripture was once established or granted as its sense, the authority of that sense was supreme. But the theory of the Reformed Theologians (Calvin, Zwingli, etc.) was that the silence of the Scripture is *prohibitory*, that this implies dissent. The Lutheran Theologians, of all times, hold that the silence of Scripture, if it does not give consent by its general letter or spirit, at least leaves the question to the great principle of Christian liberty. The whole argument, on the one side, often was: "Show me where it is commanded" (Reformed Prot.), and the whole defense: "Show me where it is forbidden" (Lutheran Prot.).

Puritanism, of which Zwingli was in general a forerunner and Romanism, like many other extremes here meet together. They meet in putting into the sphere of conscience what belongs to the sphere of liberty, only differing in their object.

The Puritan, who makes a matter of conscience as to the use (without superstition) of the cross or crucifix as an emblem, and the Romanist who makes a matter of conscience of paying superstitious reverence to that symbol, are one in principle and differ only in application.

The fundamental principle of the Lutheran Church is very clearly expressed in Luther's own words: "To forbid me as a matter of conscience what God has not forbidden, just as seriously compromises my Christian liberty, as to command me as a matter of conscience to do, what God has not commanded." On this principle the Lutheran Church feels herself at liberty to retain whatever is good in the rich treasures and sacred usages handed down in the Church, in matters not pertaining to conscience, though the Word of God does not speak of them.

There was also a difference as to the importance they attached to *the testimony of the church*. Both sides agreed that any testimony in conflict with Holy Scripture could not be accepted. Lutheran Protestantism is pre-eminently historical and conservative in her method of interpreting Scripture. She starts on the assumption that everything in the Church both of doctrine and practice, is to be regarded right, until it shall be proved by the testimony of Scripture, or by sanctified reason, to be wrong.

The Zwinglian portion of the Reformation, and much of the Pseudo-Protestantism of the modern day, starts practically with the assumption that everything in the Church, both of doctrine and of practice, is to be regarded as wrong, till it be proved by direct testimony of Scripture, to be right.

Other causes might be cited, but in these two different ways of applying the same principle lie the main causes of the division of Protestantism in the two great streams of Lutheran Protestantism, on the one hand, and Reformed Protestantism, on the other, which latter includes all the so-called historical Reformed denominations (German Reformed, Dutch Reformed, Church of England, Presbyterianism, etc.). (On 83–87 see Krauth's *Manuscript Lectures*).

Lutheran Protestantism

In the Lutheran Confessions known as the *Book of Concord*, the doctrine of the Church is presented in the Augsburg Confession (Arts. VII. and VIII.), in the Apology (Chap. IV., Arts. VII. and VIII.), Smalcald Articles (Part III., Art. XII.), Small Catechism (Art. III. of Creed), and in Large Catechism (Art. III. of Creed).

VII. of the Augsburg Confession treats of the *Inner* or *Spiritual* Essence of the Church. The Article may be thetically analyzed as follows:

1. The Church is one, holy, and perpetually abiding.

"The churches with common consent among us teach" "that one holy Church is to continue forever."

2. "The Church is the congregation of saints." The original *German* has instead of the Latin, "the assembly of all believers."

3. The external marks of the Church are 1) the pure preaching of the Gospel, and 2) the right administration of the Sacraments.

"In which the Gospel is rightly taught (*Ger.* purely preached), and the Sacraments rightly administered (*Ger.* according to the Gospel)."

4. The true unity of the Church lies in a spiritual unity.

1) Positively: "It is sufficient to agree concerning the doctrine of the Gospel and the administration of the Sacraments."

2) Negatively: "It is not necessary that human traditions, rites, or ceremonies instituted by men, should be alike everywhere."

3) Thus Scripture teaches: Eph. 4:5, 6, "There is one body, and one Spirit, even as also ye were called in one hope of your calling; one Lord, one faith, one baptism."

Art. VIII. of the A. C. treats of the Church in its Actual Appearance.

1. "The Church is properly the congregation of saints and true believers."

2. But "in this life many hypocrites and evil persons are mingled with it."

3. The sacraments are efficacious even when administered by wicked ministers.

"The Sacraments and the Word are effectual, by reason of the institution and commandment of Christ, though they be delivered by evil men."

In Chap. IV. of the Apology, on Arts. VII. and VIII. of the A. C., it is noticed that the Romanists condemn Art. VII. of A.C., especially for affirming that "the Church is the congregation of saints." The Apology goes on to say, "for this reason, we added the eighth Article, lest anyone may think that we separate the wicked and hypocrites from the outward fellowship of the Church, or that we deny efficacy to the sacraments when they are administered by hypocrites or wicked men."

We may analyze the discussion as follows:

1. The definition of the Church (§ 1–29).

1) Hypocrites and wicked men have only outward fellowship with the Church (§ 1–3).

2) Sacraments are efficacious even when administered by wicked men (§ 3, 4).

3) The Church is principally a spiritual fellowship of faith and in the Holy Ghost (§ 5).

4) The outward marks of this fellowship are two, *a*) the pure doctrine of the Gospel, and *b*) the right administration of the Sacraments (§5, 6).

5) Paul defines the Church in exactly the same way, and also adds the outward marks, the Word and Sacraments, Eph. 5:25–27 (§ 7).

6) The true definition of the Church is, the congregation of saints (§ 8).

7) This article is very comforting and highly necessary (§ 9 11).

8) The Church is not properly an outward polity, but the Church is the true people of God, regenerated by the Holy Ghost (§ 12–14).

9) The Church is distinguished from "the people of the Law" (§ 14, 15).

10) The Church is distinguished from the kingdom of the devil (§ 16).

11) Wicked men, though outwardly members of the Church, are not the Church (§ 17–19).

12) This is not a Platonic dream, for the Church really exists, and consists in "the truly believing and righteous men scattered throughout the world" (§ 20).

13) The external marks of this Church are two, "the pure doctrine of the Gospel, and the Sacraments."

14) "And this Church is properly the pillar of the truth" (1 Tim. 3:15), "for it retains the pure Gospel, 'the foundation,' *i.e.*, the true knowledge of Christ and faith (1 Cor. 3:12)" (§ 20).

15) "The Church consists of those persons in whom there is a true knowledge and confession of faith and truth" (§ 21, 22).

16) The definition of the Church as given by Rome is not a definition of the Church of Christ, but of the papal kingdom, and of the kingdom of Antichrist, pictured by Daniel (11:36, 37) (§ 23–27).

The Scripture doctrine, then, is this (§ 28, 29):

a) "The Church, properly so called, is the congregation of saints, who truly believe the Gospel of Christ, and have the Holy Ghost."

b) In this life many hypocrites and wicked men are members of the Church according to the fellowship of outward signs.

c) "The fact that the sacraments are administered by the unworthy, does not detract from their efficacy, because on account of the call of the Church, they represent the person of Christ, and do not represent their own persons, as Christ testifies (Luke 10:16): "He that heareth you heareth me." "

2. Of the unity of the Church (§ 30–46).

1) The true unity of the Church consists in spiritual unity (§ 30. 31). "They are one harmonious Church, who believe in one Christ, who have one Gospel, one Spirit, one faith, the same sacraments."

2) "The true unity of the Church is not injured by dissimilar rites instituted by men" (§ 32–37).

3) The demand of Rome that we must observe human rites and ordinances to establish the unity of the Church is contrary to the doctrine of the Apostles. "The Apostles did not wish us to believe that such rites are necessary for righteousness before God"; "they did not wish to place righteousness and sin in the observance of days, food, and the like. Yea, Paul calls such opinions doctrines of devils" (1 Tim. 4:1) (§ 38–46).

3. On Art. VIII. the Apology calls attention to the fact that Rome did not object to this Article.

1) "Sacraments are efficacious even though distributed by wicked ministers" (§ 47–49).

2) "It is lawful for Christians to use civil ordinances" (§ 50).

3) The treatment in the Smalcald Articles is very brief.

1. The Church of Rome is not the Church (§ 1).

2. The Church consists of saints and believers (§ 2).

"For, thank God, today a child seven years old knows what the Church is, viz., saints, believers and lambs who hear the voice of the Shepherd. For the children repeat: I believe in one holy, Catholic or Christian Church."

3. The holiness of the Church "consists in the Word of God and true faith" (§ 3).

In the Large Catechism (Art. III. of the Creed) special attention is given to the explanation of the expression 'congregation of saints" and the discussion is summed up as follows:

1. "I believe that there is upon earth a holy assembly and congregation of pure saints, under one head, even Christ, called together by the Holy Ghost in one faith, one mind and understanding, with manifold gifts, yet one in love, without sect or schisms" ... (§ 51).

2. "Until the last day the Holy Ghost abides with the holy congregation or Christian people" (§ 53).

3. "By means of this congregation the Holy Ghost brings us to Christ and teaches and preaches to us the Word, whereby He works and promotes sanctification" (§ 53).

4. "Outside of this Christian Church, where the Gospel is not, there is no forgiveness, as also there can be no sanctification" (§ 56).

Although the doctrine of the Church was not directly discussed in the *Formula of Concord*, there are several important statements confirming the doctrine as stated in the earlier Confessions. We need only refer to three passages, bearing on the *unity* of the Church.

For thorough, permanent unity in the Church, it is before all things necessary that we have a comprehensive, unanimously approved summary and form of the pure doctrine of God's Word (*Introd. to Sol. Decl.* § 1, 2).

"For the maintenance of pure doctrine, and for thorough, permanent, godly unity in the Church, it is necessary not only that pure, wholesome doctrine be rightly presented, but also that the opponents who teach otherwise be reproved" (1 Tim. 3:2, 15; 2 Tim. 3:16; Tit. 1:9; John 10:12; Jer. 15:19). (*Introd. to Sol. Decl.*, § 14).

Uniformity of ceremonies are not necessary for true unity.

"We believe, teach and confess that no Church should condemn another because one has less or more external ceremonies not commanded by God than the other, if otherwise there is agreement among them in doctrine and all its articles, as also in the right use of the holy sacraments, according to the well-known saying: 'Disagreement in fasting does not destroy agreement in faith'" (*Epit. Chap.* X. 7). (The quotation is from Irenæus.)

Outline of Dr. Krauth's Lecture on Art. VII. of Augsburg Confession

Outline of Lecture on Art. VII. of Augsburg Confession. (Based on Dr. Krauth's *Lecture in Manuscript*).

1. "Unto the true unity of the Church" two things are necessary, 1) "It is sufficient to agree concerning the doctrine of the Gospel," and 2) "the administration of the sacraments."

2. The proof passage cited, Eph. 4:5, says *one faith*, and without this *one faith* all the other parts of the unity are impossible; and with this *one faith* all the other parts of the unity come as a matter of course. It is the *one faith* which knits us into the "one body", one faith which is the gift of the "one Spirit"; it is the one faith looking out into the future, which is the ground of the "one hope" of our calling; it is the one faith which rests on the "one Lord", and unites us with Him; it is the one faith to which the "one Baptism" offers its grace, and seals its blessings, and hence it is the one faith which makes us children indeed of "one God and Father of all".

3. The second mark of unity is that the sacraments are rightly administered, *i.e.*, as the Gospel commands.

4. What the teaching of the Gospel is concerning the Sacrament of initiation, Baptism, we learn from Matt. 28:18–20, where our Lord represents it as a constituent element of unity of the Church, that we be baptized "into the name of the Father and of the Son and of the Holy Ghost."

5. Note *first*, that our Savior grounds the ministry upon His own supreme power as Mediator, intrinsically His as God, and given to Him as man, "all authority hath been given to me in heaven and on earth". The ministry rests upon the supreme authority of our Lord.

6. Note *secondly*, that from Himself as the center and as the result of this authority they are to go forth. The ministry is a moving, aggressive, progressing office, not waiting to be sought, but of a missionary and seeking activity.

7. Note *thirdly*, that they were to make disciples, not to found monarchies. "Make ye disciples" indicates the process and the

result. They were to bear the whole energy of the Gospel as Word and Sacrament, and by it to make men disciples.

8. *Fourthly*, the basis of the making of a disciple was to be the baptism of men. The maturing of disciples was to be the ampler teaching of the truth. "To make a disciple" includes two things, 1) baptizing and 2) teaching, and the baptism is put first. The entire structure of the sentence, so far from favoring the per version that of necessity instruction must precede baptism, asserts directly the contrary. Some instruction of adults preceded their baptism, enough to enable them intelligently to receive baptism, but the great body of instruction in their case, and the entire instruction in the case of their infant children, followed it. Almost the entire mass of the Apostolic instruction as given in the Epistles is designed for those already baptized.

9. The baptismal commission of our Lord covers the whole essential unity of the Church. It directly asserts all the main points of Art. VII. of the A. C.

1) Both teach that there is to be one Church.

2) Both declare that this one Church is to remain "even unto the end of the world" (Matt. 28:20).

3) Both teach that the saints are to be gathered, made disciples of, and that among them the Gospel is to be purely preached and the sacraments rightly administered. "Whatsover I command you" means *what* I have commanded and *as* I have commanded (Acts 28:20).

10. That the Sacrament of Baptism is essential to the unity of the Church is further seen by noting how strongly the New Testament guards against two antithetical errors:

1) Against the "opus operatum" as if he that believeth not, and is baptized, shall be saved; and

2) the more plausible opposite perversion, as if he that believeth, and is not baptized, shall be saved.

3) Our Lord attests the truth over against both these errors, when He lays it down as the law of the kingdom that "he that believeth and is baptized shall be saved" (Mark 16:16).

4) No one is to connect and read a *not* either with "believeth" or with "baptized."

11. There are many Scripture passages which prove that Baptism rightly administered is a necessary characteristic of the one Church, and essential to its true unity.

1) In Acts 2:38 in answer to the question asked by convicted men, "What shall we do?" the Apostle Peter said, "Repent" and there the answer of many moderns would end; but the Apostle adds, "and be baptized every one of you in the name of Jesus Christ unto the remission of your sins; and ye shall receive the gifts of the Holy Ghost."

2) In Acts 22:16, Ananias, after having restored Saul's sight, directs him to be baptized, and wash away his sins, calling on the name of the Lord.

3) In 1 Cor. 12:13, "For in one Spirit were we all baptized into one body... and were made to drink of one Spirit," Baptism is declared to be the sole ordinary instrument of the Holy Ghost whereby men are inserted into Christ's own body.

4) From Gal. 3:27, "For as many of you as were baptized into Christ did put on Christ," we learn that Baptism in the fullness of its blessing, rightly received, unites us to Christ, and invests us with all that Christ brings. Over against the idea of "*opus operatum,*" that Baptism saves without faith, Gal. 3:26 says, "Ye are all sons of God, through faith, in Christ Jesus," and then proves this by the following verse (Gal. 3:27), a most manifest proof that Holy Baptism offers to faith that by which the believer is actually invested with Christ. For by baptism one becomes a member of the body of Christ, is incorporated into the *permanent* communion of Christ, as well as into His means and effects of grace, whereby he receives the conditions for a progressive development of personality. Even to a believer, who by faith in Christ Jesus has become God's child (Gal. 3:26), baptism is to be regarded as the means which conveys, seals, and invests a man with the grace symbolized in its external part.

5) In 1 Pet. 3:21, "which also after a true likeness doth now save you, even baptism," Baptism, in its true function is made parallel to the flood. It is the instrument of separation. It is that which while it implies the ruin of those who receive not its benefits, works the salvation of those who receive it aright.

6) All these passages show that baptism rightly administered is a necessary characteristic of the one Church.

12. Equally clear is it, that the Lord's Supper is an essential mark of the true unity of the Church.

1) 1 Cor. 11:24, "this do in remembrance of me," that is in commemoration of me. That cannot be Christ's one Church which does not do in commemoration of Him what He commands to be done. The Lord's Supper is no temporary mark of the Church, but is to abide to the end of time, "till He come," 1 Cor. 11:26.

2) The whole argument of 1 Cor. 11:20–29 is designed to show that it is the duty of the Christian to partake aright of this Holy Sacrament.

3) No part of the Church Catholic ever doubted the permanent obligation of the Holy Supper.

4) Just in proportion as the love of the Church to her Lord was fervent and her devotion pure, was the frequent celebration of the Lord's Supper. In the Early Church, and in the first glow of love and devotion in the days of the Reformation, the Lord's Supper was a constituent element of every chief service on the Lord's Day.

5) Our chief service in the "Church Book," modeled as it is upon the ancient services of our Church, and of the Church Catholic, implies the communion as an integral part of the Morning Service, and without the celebration of the Lord's Supper, it is, at best, but a beautiful fragment.

13. The Sacraments of Baptism and the Lord's Supper, however, are not simply to be retained in some shape, but in order to be marks of the Church, they are to be rightly administered (see 3 *above*).

14. In a right administration of a Sacrament *two* things are involved:

1) The right elements conformably to the commands of the Gospel, shall be used—in Baptism, water; in the Lord's Supper, bread and wine. Baptism is not to be administered with wine or sand, or any other thing except water; the Lord's Supper is not to be administered with water, or infusions of fruits, whether called wine or not, but that which alone is true wine, namely the product of the fruit of the vine.

2) The appointed Word is to be used, Christ's own words of institution being the guide in both cases. They are to be

used, not in a mere repetition of the history of what He said, but in His name and by His authority, and thus used they consecrate. If in Baptism the administrator says in the place of the divine words, "I baptize thee in the name of the Creator, the Redeemer and the Sanctifier," there is no baptism. If in the Lord's Supper the administrator ignores the divine words, and in place of them says, "This bread is a symbol of Christ's body," there is no Supper of the Lord. You can no more make a divine sacrament with human words, than you can make a golden goblet out of lead.

15. The organic center of the unity of the Church is her *faith*.

1) One faith, not two faiths, still less many faiths.

2) Where there are two divisions in the form of distinct churches or denominations, they either make a question of faith out of what is not such, or one or the other is wrong, (if indeed both be not wrong), and so far as either is wrong, it is relatively out of the unity of the Church.

3) There cannot be two conflicting divisions in the Church unless there is schism or heresy somewhere.

4) It is not primarily practice that is involved, nor discipline, but the "doctrine of the Gospel."

5) By the doctrine of the Gospel is meant the inmost truth which connects itself with the person, office, and world-redeeming work of our Lord Jesus Christ, and our participation in the blessings of them, through the Holy Ghost, in living faith, by means of the pure Word and Sacraments.

16. The Augsburg Confession (Art. VII.) carefully, in most exact language, defines what is necessary to the *true* unity of the Church.

1) The Confessors speak of a *true* unity, not of a spurious, specious, and illusive unity, but of a real, scriptural, internal, and *true* unity.

2) The expression "it is enough", "it is sufficient" "to agree", etc., is very suggestive. There are many things that grace a real unity, that naturally and almost inevitably follow from it, but which yet are not an essential part of it, *e.g.*, that the Church has one common government, that individual

congregations represent themselves in one general body, that they sustain each other's discipline, that they have one common order of Worship, etc., but these things, beautiful and desirable as they are, are not the essentials of unity. They might exist where there is no unity, and unity might exist without them.

3) The Confessors are very careful in the use of terms. They speak of *unity*, not uniformity.

4) They are not satisfied with defining *true unity*, positively, but they characterize it also negatively, over against false unity. "It is not necessary that human traditions, rites, or ceremonies, instituted by men, should be everywhere alike."

17. This negative statement was aimed primarily at the false theories and practices of the Church of Rome. Let us first consider *Human Traditions*.

1) Traditions are either good, or bad, or indifferent, or they may be indifferent or good in themselves and yet be abused so as to be incidentally bad.

2) Now the observance of any of these traditions is not necessary to that true internal unity of which the Confession speaks.

3) The bad tend to destroy it; the indifferent, in due bounds, effect very little, out of due bounds, they mar the unity; the good grace it, may even aid and promote it, but they are not essential to it. The unity existed before them, it would exist were all the good traditions swept away.

4) The essence of unity is purely a thing of God and exists apart from all human traditions of whatever kind.

18. Let us also consider *Human Rites and Ceremonies*.

1) Rites are either human or divine. It is of the former the Confession speaks. The divine rites, especially of Baptism and the Lord's Supper, are essential to the true unity of the Church, but the *human* rites are not.

2) Like the human traditions on which they rest, the rites or ceremonies instituted by men are either bad, indifferent, or good.

3) In our day much is said about Ritualism, often in ignorance of what Ritualism is.

4) If Ritualism means the observance of due rites, then all the Christians except the Friends are Ritualists in principle, and even the Friends are in their very unritualism most tenaciously ritualistic. They make a stringent rite of the absence of Ritualism.

5) It is therefore not a question whether due rites shall be observed, but what are due rites.

6) By Ritualism is now generally meant an undue observance of rites either in kind or in extent.

7) The use of a prescribed service or form of common prayer is not Ritualism in this unfavorable sense. Such a service was used in the O.T. times, as well as in the N.T. times, and in the Ancient Church.

8) The fixed forms of Worship, now in use in the Lutheran Church, in most of its elements originated near the Apostolic Times, probably under the direction of the disciples of the Apostles themselves.

9) All the original Reformers of every school, Calvin and Zwingle being no exceptions, used and in many cases prepared forms of service.

19. Ritualism exists in an unfavorable sense:

1) When rites are used which in themselves are superstitious, *e.g.*, the adoration of the bread and the wine in the Lord's Supper. Rome gives to bread and wine the worship due to the Creator. The Roman Catholic does not mean idolatry. Granting his theory of transubstantiation he is not an idolator, but if his theory be wrong, his worship is idolatry.

2) When rites in themselves indifferent or innocent are used for the purpose of setting forth false doctrine. *a*) The sign or figure of the cross is in itself a mere memorial, whether it is a stamp on a book, or an emblem on a seal, whether it be fixed on a church, or signed on the forehead of a child, or made with the hand in the air, and so understood, the sign is in itself innocent, useful, and suggestive. But when to the superstitious certain virtue is supposed to be connected with the sign, then the use of it is idolatrous. *b*) Statuary and painting, innocent in themselves, may be abused for the purpose of saint worship, and thus become pernicious. *c*) Even the brazen serpent made by God's command, when it became

the object of idolatrous worship, received a contemptuous name and was broken to pieces (2 Kings 18:4). *d*) The mere abuse to superstition does not, however, take away the right use,—(the sun has been worshipped, the Bible has been used in fortune-telling, the Lord's Prayer has been employed in witchcraft, the elements of the Lord's Supper have been carried away for sorcery). *e*) When the use may easily lead to the abuse, the simplest way to correct the evil is to abandon the thing altogether.

3) When rites and ceremonies in themselves good, or even divine, are used in excess. *a*) The use of the *Kyrie* is good, but to employ it nine times in succession (as Rome does), is in excess; *b*) to use the Apostles' Creed or the Lord's prayer ten times in one service is ritualistic excess; *c*) to use too many hymns, or an excessive amount of a particular hymn (some of the old hymns have twenty to fifty stanzas) is ritualistic; *d*) sermons too long, and prayers too long, tend to ritualistic excess.

4) The spirit of ritualism may exist in the form of violent anti-ritualism. *a*) This is the case whenever rites in themselves innocent are opposed, not on the ground of abuse, or of excess, but as if they were matters in the sphere of conscience, and not the subject of Christian liberty; *b*) How much excitement is produced by a few Churches going to ritualistic extremes, but not one word of reprobation for the carelessness and indecency of the opposite extreme; *c*) There is a popery of Romanism, and there is a popery of ultra-Protestantism; *d*) The greatest danger in this country lies in ultra-Protestantism.

20. Over against Romish errors about unity in rites and ceremonies, instituted by man, the whole Lutheran Reformation is a long protest.

21. Not only does the Lutheran Church attest that she has no compromise with Rome in her errors, but equally clear is her testimony that she has no sympathy with the ultraism and extravagance of sectarianism.

22. All our real difficulties in the so-called Protestant Evangelical Churches as to unity are derived from one source;

there is somewhere and in some respects, on the part of some, a lack of the one faith.

23. The *one faith* is the organic center of the Church.

1) The Word of God reveals one system of doctrine. Hence no co-ordinate conflicting systems can be allowed as of equal validity in the Church.

2) This one system of doctrine is ascertainable. Our Protestant principle is that the Holy Scripture is clear in all articles of Faith.

3) The various denominations claim to have ascertained that system of doctrine, and they account for the defects in the views of others, not by the *want* of clearness in the revelation, but by the blindness and infirmity of man.

4) On our common admission they and we are responsible for the attaining of the true doctrine of the Gospel.

5) False doctrine, whether regarded as heresy in the sense of a deviation from the faith of the Gospel, or heresy considered as a schismatic division apart from the ground of faith, is treated in Scripture, not as a misfortune, but as a crime, a work of the flesh.

6) The various Protestant denominations do not have a unity of faith, and yet the Scriptures declare that unity is an essential element of the Church.

7) We dare not say, though we need it and have it not, yet as we cannot get it, that we must do the best we can without, and cover the chasm with charity. This will only increase a hopeless schism in the name of charity.

24. The first thing necessary to bring about unity of doctrine is the most thorough honesty and clearness in the statement of doctrine.

1) No real harmony can be brought about by mere acquiescence in forms of words, which are indeed accepted by different parties, but in different senses.

2) Nothing is gained by assuming and insisting that differences are not real, when they are real.

25. To seek for the truth and to recognize the truth when found, is the only way to bring about unity.

1) These two tendencies, indifference to truth and a charity which aims at unity without the one faith, are doing infinite mischief throughout our whole land.

2.) These tendencies cannot permanently co-exist with strong convictions, and are largely the cause of the destructive negative movements of the day.

3) Rationalism and infidelity in general are the offspring of the indifferentism and unionism of the day,—of the concealments, ambiguities, and trifling with truth.

IN THE HISTORY OF THE LUTHERAN CHURCH

The Teaching of our Older Dogmaticians

The Teaching of Luther.

As early as 1519, Luther maintained at Leipzig, in opposition to the authority of the Pope and the Church of Rome "that there is one holy Church universal which is the whole body of the predestined;" later, however, he maintained more correctly, that the Church is "the communion of saints." See especially the "Large Catechism," already referred to *above*.

The Church is, according to Luther, nothing more nor less than "the congregation (*gemeine*) of the Saints." It exists and can exist only where the gospel is preached and the sacraments rightly administered. By these, as by outward signs, the Christian congregation is recognized. "Wherever the Gospel is, there must also be a holy Christian Church."

This Church as the community of existing believers possess and dispenses the means of grace, and stands related to the individual believer as his mother. It conceives, bears, and trains up an innumerable host of children through the Gospel and the Holy Spirit. To this community of believers or the Church we must go to secure the forgiveness of sins.

Not all the baptized truly remain members of the Church. When any one becomes an impenitent sinner and an enemy of the truth, he is no longer a true member of the Church, but only in name.

The Church is in her essence principally invisible, inasmuch as it involves an article of faith. Luther says: "Is the article true, 'I believe in a holy Christian Church?' then it follows that no one can *see* or *feel* the Holy Christian Church; no one consequently can say, Lo, here it is, or there it is, for what we believe is not an object of sight or sense, perception; and again, what a man sees or perceives, that he does not believe."

As at the beginning of the Reformation it was necessary to give prominence to the *invisible* essence of the Church over against the sensuousness of the Roman Catholic conception, so at a later period, in opposition to the Donatistic and fanatical errors of the Anabaptists, it was necessary to give prominence to the *visibility* of the Church in her outward manifestation, as seen in the statement of Melanchthon.

Melanchthon in his "Loci" of 1535, and yet more in 1543, gives special prominence to the truth that the Church is in some sense visible, and that we are not to dream that the elect are anywhere but in this visible Church. In this aspect he defines the Church, not as "the communion of Saints," but as "the assembly of the called." "As often as we think of the Church, we contemplate an assembly of the called, which is the visible Church, nor are we to dream that any of the elect are elsewhere than in this visible assembly... The visible Church is the assembly of those who embrace the Gospel of Christ and rightly use the Sacraments, in which Church God, through the ministry of the Gospel, is efficacious and regenerates many unto eternal life."

The definition of the Church given by our older Lutheran Dogmaticians.

Chemnitz (*d.* 1586) lays stress upon the visibility of the Church. He says: "It ought to be known to us, and for this reason it is defined to be the visible assembly of those who embrace the Gospel of Christ."

When the controversy with Rome became more pressing, our Dogmaticians bring more into relief the invisible Church, and allow the element of its essential visibleness to fall into the background.

Hutter (*d.* 1616) says: "The visible Church is the assembly of the called (*i.e.*, the Church in the wide sense, improperly so-called); the invisible Church is the whole assembly of true believers and saints (*i.e.*, the Church strictly and properly so-called)." The former is called the Church only "by synecdoche—

that is attributed to the whole, made up of good and bad, which strictly belongs only to a part."

There are not two churches, but only two sides of the same Church. The true visible Church is one with the true invisible Church. Gerhard (*d.* 1637) says: "We by no means introduce two Churches opposed one to the other, but we say that one and the same Church, is in diverse respects, both visible and invisible."

Of the three expressions, "Assembly of the called," "Congregation of Saints," "Congregation of the elect," it best to use the second as the true definition of the Church.

1) The Church is "the congregation of saints who truly believe in the Gospel of Christ, and have the Holy Ghost" (Apology IV, 28).

2) "It is preferable to define the Church as the congregation of saints and true believers, than of the elect" (*Gerhard*).

Quenstedt (*d.* 1688) gives the Scriptural proof that the Church is "the congregation of saints" (quoted by Schmid):

"1) The Church is called the mystical body of Christ (Rom. 12:5; 1 Cor. 10:17; 12:27; Eph. 1:23; Col. 1:18);

"2) The Church is the mother of true believers (Gal. 4:26), of the Sons of God (John 1:12; 3:6), who are led by the Spirit of God (Rom. 8:14), and are the heirs of Christ (Rom. 8:17);

"3) The Church is Christ's fold (John 10:1, 27, 28);

"4) Prophets and apostles frequently ascribe such praises to the Church as cannot be referred to the entire assembly of the called, which embraces good and evil, wheat and tares (Matt. 13:25), good and bad fish, sheep and goats (Matt. 3:12; 13:47, 49; John 10:1). Therefore that must be termed the Church, properly and accurately so called, to which these praises and attributes mainly and immediately belong."

The Scientific Presentation of our older Lutheran Dogmaticians.

The *Attributes* of the Church pertain strictly only to the Church properly so-called—to the invisible Church. They belong to the visible Church only by *synecdoche*, attributing to it what belongs only to a part.

The Church is *militant* and *triumphant*. "The Church is called *militant*, because under the standard of Christ it fights throughout this life against 1) the devil, Eph. 6:10, 11; 1 Pet. 5:8, 9;

2) the world, 1 John 5:4; 3) and the flesh, Rom. 7:14; Gal. 5:17."
(*Gerhard.*) With respect to the life to come the Church is called
triumphant, because "being transferred to heavenly rest, she is
liberated from the labor and the toil of conflict and the danger of
defeat" (Rev. 2:10; 4:4; 7:9). (*Gerhard.*) The Church as a whole will
not be finally triumphant until the end of the world.

The Church is said to be 1) *one and undivided,* because there is
only *one Head,* even Christ, to whom all are united, and only *one*
faith through which they can be saved; 2) *one and no more,*
inasmuch as the Church universal is the assembly of *all believers*
united by faith to Christ, as the Head; and because this Church,
from its first beginning, has continued by a constant succession of
believers to the present time, and will always continue until the
end of time (After *Hollaz*).

"The Church is said to be *holy,* 1) because Christ, its Head, is
holy (Heb. 7:26), who makes the Church partaker of His holiness
(John 17:19); 2) because it is called by a holy calling and separated
from the world (2 Tim. 1:9); 3) because the Word of God,
committed to it, is holy (Rom. 3:2); 4) because the Holy Ghost in
this assembly sanctifies believers by applying to them, through
faith, Christ's holiness, working inner renewal and holiness in
their hearts, and awakening in them the desire of perfect
holiness" (*Gerhard* quoted in *Schmid*).

The Church is called *Catholic* or *Universal* 1) *with respect to its
properties,* because of its doctrine and faith, in so far as it
professes the faith that the whole body of believers has *at all
times* professed; 2) *with respect to its extent,* because of its being
spread over the entire globe; 3) *with respect to its aim,* for the
doctrine and faith it professes is for all men, and has been
entrusted to the Church, that the Gospel might be preached for
the salvation of all (After *Hollaz*).

"The Church is called *Apostolic,* partly because it was planted
by the Apostles, and partly because it has embraced and been
built upon the doctrine handed down by the Apostles, 'being built
upon the foundation of the Apostles and prophets'" (*Hollaz*
quoted in *Schmid*).

It is only of the invisible Church that the proposition holds
good, *extra ecclesiam nulla salus,* "Out of the Church is no
Salvation." This is but another way of saying, "No one will be
saved who does not believe." Gerhard says: "It is necessary for

every one of those who are to be saved to be a living member and true citizen of the *Universal* (Catholic or Christian) *and Apostolic Church;* and those who are outside of the Church are, necessarily, aliens from God, from Christ, from the benefits of the heavenly Kingdom, and the hope of eternal salvation. This is proved 1) by Eph. 2:12, 13; 4:16; 5:8; 1 Pet. 2:9; Rev. 22:15; 21:8; 2) by the peculiar benefits conferred by the Church, such as regeneration, renewal etc.; for since these have no place outside of the Church, there also cannot be salvation outside of the Church" (Quoted by *Schmid*).

Our Dogmaticians also distinguish between the *Church Universal* and particular Churches. After *Quenstedt* we may make the following distinctions (Quoted in *Schmid*):

1) The Church is said to be *Universal,* 1) with respect to place, and 2) with respect to time.

2) The *Church Universal, considered absolutely,* or with respect to both time and place, is the general assembly of true believers, whom God, from the beginning of the world to its end, has called and will call, through the preaching of the Word, out of all peoples and nations, to the actual participation in spiritual and heavenly blessings.

3) The *Church Universal,* considered relatively, is the assembly of all true believers, who at any one time, as at the present day, everywhere continue in one and the same communion of faith, grace, love and salvation.

4) A particular Church is an assembly, not of all, but of some believers, called in a certain place to partake of salvation, and persevering in inner spiritual communion.

5) Particular Churches are diverse in time and place.
Further explication of what is meant by a *particular Church.*

1) A *particular Church,* preeminently and properly such in the Bible sense, is not a denomination, sect or schism, but a Christian congregation.

2) The modern conception of particular Churches as denominations, diverse in doctrines, organized on the basis of that difference, is wholly unknown in the New Testament.

3) A denomination in this sense would be called in the N.T. a sect or schism.

4) The Lutheran Church is not a particular Church in this sense, but only in this, that she embraces in her communion a number of pure particular congregations in the N.T. sense, in the unity of a common confession of the truth, and she repudiates the idea that any pure Church can be a particular Church in the sense of being one of a set of warring sects, equally legitimate.

5) When we say that the Lutheran Church, in the larger sense, is a particular Church, we only mean that she does not (as Rome does) claim to contain all the members of the Church universal, but believes and confesses that, by the grace of God, living believers are found in all denominations of the Christian Church, even perhaps, in exceptional cases, in some of the most heterodox.

6) Even the whole Church on earth, at any one time, is not the *universal* Church, but only a fraction of it, and in this sense *particular*, the Church of a particular time over against the Church of all times.

With reference to doctrine and confession, the visible Church of the Called is divided into the *true* or *pure* Church, and the *false* or *impure* Church.

"The *true or pure Church* is the assembly of men in which all things necessary to be believed for salvation, and to be done for attaining holiness of life, are clearly taught from God's Word, without the mixture of any hurtful errors, and the Sacraments are rightly administered according to the institution of Christ, and thus spiritual Sons of God are begotten, who, through true faith, are united to Christ the Head, and in Him are made one body" (*Hollaz* in *Schmid*).

"*A false or impure Church* is an assembly of men, in which the doctrine of faith is publicly proclaimed from the Word of God, with a mixture of errors and corruptions, and the Sacraments are indeed administered, yet not distributed in that manner, and for that end, in and for which they were instituted by Christ" (*Hollaz* in *Schmid*).

Further elucidation of the topic. (After Hollaz, Gerhard, Krauth.)
1) The falseness of a Church is obviously a relative thing; one Church may be much more impure than another.

2) The purity of a Church cannot, in the same sense as falseness and impurity, be said to be relative.

3) The relative purity of the true Church can only be relative as regards that Church herself, in different stages of the divine development.

4) A pure or true Church holds throughout the one faith, and all pure churches, and even all impure churches, so far as they retain any elements of purity, hold one and the same faith.

5) Churches cannot be one in spite of different faiths, but only in consequence of, and so far as they are united in holding one faith.

6) Salvation is possible to the individual in some of the false or impure churches, because God's Word is there and His sacraments are there; and although both Word and sacraments may be so obscured as to make salvation difficult to any one, and actually to cause many to fall short of it, still others may be saved.

7) Whenever Baptism is rightly administered, though the Word outside of that Baptism be perverted, and the Lord's Supper be mutilated, salvation is possible to some.

8) The marks of the true and pure visible Church are the pure teaching, especially by the preaching of the Word of God and the legitimate administration of the Sacraments.

9) Under the preaching of the Word is embraced all public setting forth of the doctrine of the faith, especially in an official form, receiving general recognition.

10) Whether the doctrine of a particular Church is to be considered pure or impure is to be determined from the symbols or public confessions put forth in the name of the whole Church, or approved by the whole Church.

11) This doctrine of a particular Church is not to be gathered from the opinions or writings of this or that man, however eminent.

12) The works of the standard theologians of a Church are, however, of great value in the interpretation of the confessions of the Church.

13) If we accept this definition of the marks of the Church, the deduction is inevitable, that the Roman Catholic Church is neither true nor catholic.

14) The Christian Church which adheres to the Augsburg Confession is a true Church in a supreme and peculiar sense and degree. She embraces the Catholic doctrine and hence is in

quality Catholic, although with respect to amplitude she is not the Catholic Church, but a particular Church.

Dr. Krauth (*Cons. Ref.*): "As genuine Lutheranism is most Biblical among systems which professedly ground themselves on the supreme authority of God's word; as it is most evangelical among the systems that magnify our Savior's grace; so is our Church at once most truly Catholic among all churches which acknowledge that the faith of God's people is one, and most truly Protestant among all bodies claiming to be Protestant. She is the mother of all Protestantism. Her confession at Augsburg is the first official statement of Scriptural doctrine and usage ever issued against Romish heresy and corruption. Her confessions are a wall of adamant against Romanism... The anathemas of the Council of Trent are almost all leveled at our Church."

A distinction is further drawn by our Dogmaticians between the *Synthetic* or *Collective* Church and the *Representative* Church.

Hollaz says: "The *Synthetic* Church is the Church taken collectively, consisting of teachers and hearers, joined by the bond of the same faith, and is called the *Collective* Church in distinction from the *Representative Church*, which is an assembly of teachers solemnly assembled to decide questions concerning the doctrine of faith and Christian morals" (*Examen*, 1266).

Again: "The word *church* in the Scriptures is sometimes, by synecdoche (of the whole for a part), used to designate a convention of teachers and deputies of the Church, who represent the synthetic Church, and whatever they do in the public name by the power granted to them, that is held as ratified by the other members of the Church, and is regarded as something to be done, or as having been done by all. Thus the word *church* is taken in Matt. 18:17, where Christ says, 'Tell it unto the Church,' meaning a representative assembly of the synthetical Church, whether in council, synod, or consistory" (*Examen*, 1266).

Again: "The *Representative* Church is an assembly of teachers representing in its own mode the synthetic Church. For the *Synthetic* Church is represented by its ministry and by a council, or a synod.... In councils are assembled the teachers and delegates of churches to whom has been committed by the whole communion of believers the power of investigating and deciding in regard to the public interpretation of doctrine in doubtful and controverted points and in regard to ceremonies tending to good order in the Church, as also the power of correcting open sins" (*Examen*, 1313).

Quenstedt: "The name of the *Representative* Church is given to an assembly of religious teachers and deputies of the Church, whether of all the churches or singly, which assembly represents the Synthetic Church and offers, as it were, an image and compend of the Church. This assembly of teachers and bishops is sometimes called a Council, or, after the Greek, a Synod, and to distinguish it from civil conventions the term *ecclesiastical* is added. The whole visible Church is represented in a just and legitimate council, which offers, as it were, an image or compend of the whole Church."

Buddeus: "Both the ministry and synods are sometimes called the representative Church, because through them in a certain respect the Church is represented. For in Synods, where the delegates of a number of churches are present, each one represents that particular Church by which he is sent. As a matter of course, when a number of delegates are present they take the place of many churches."

This representative character may belong to smaller bodies; a congregation may represent itself, as it does in its council; a few congregations may be represented in a conference; a large number in a Synod; Synods may be represented in a general Synod; or the whole Lutheran Church on earth might be represented in a real œcumenical council.

The Church ought to be represented in Synods or Councils by lay delegates as well as by clerical delegates. If she have but one class, she must be represented by the clergy, inasmuch as the ministers of the Gospel are already called of God through the Church to represent the Church.

The three estates in the Church, the triple hierarchical order, embracing the ecclesiastical, the political, and the domestic estate, will be discussed under the office of the ministry.

The Later Development of the Doctrine of the Church

The later development of the doctrine of the Church

This development passes through the various stages of enfeebling and dissolution, and then of re-strengthening and restoration, common to other doctrines. The doctrine of the

Church, however, in certain respects fails to reach its old strength and internal harmony.

In contradiction to religious indifference and unbelief, which depreciated the idea and authority of the Church in every sense, *Spener* (*d.* 1705) strove to counteract this disintegrating tendency by awakening the laity; but Pietisms ought mainly to satisfy personal religious wants, and laid the main stress on the small religious communions within the Church. The piety emphasized, displayed itself in a narrow, legal character, somewhat related to the Reformed idea.

Rationalism considered the Church as a purely human organization, at best only an institution for the moral culture of men, and denied that Jesus ever contemplated the formation of a Church.

Supernaturalism was fond of speaking of virtuous men, not Christians, as members of the invisible Church, or if it speaks more correctly of the Church, it yet was lacking in a proper consciousness of what the Church is.

Kant and his school substituted for the Church natural religion and moral fellowship.

Of great influence was the teaching of *Schleiermacher* (1768–1834), who restored to the Church much of its significance by giving to all theological science a relation to it. According to him the Church embraces everything which has been placed in the world through the work of redemption. Through the Church are revealed all the operations of grace upon individuals. It is itself a communion of the regenerated revivified by the Holy Ghost. Inasmuch as the Church cannot shape itself out of the world without having an influence exercised upon it by the world,—it comes to pass that the Church establishes for itself a distinction between the visible and the invisible Church.

According to the philosopher *Hegel* (1770–1831), the State is the actualizing of the moral idea. If this idea were attained the Church would no longer have a right to individual existence.

Rothe (1790–1867), occupies a position midway between Schleiermacher and Hegel. He held, that in the true moral development, civil society is in itself a religious community. It is the vocation of the Church to infuse itself more and more into the State, and as the State becomes perfect the Church disappears in proportion. This gradual solution of the Church in the State can take place only by the State becoming a religious body, a kingdom of God. Rothe comes to the conclusion that the Episcopate, as a necessary substitute for the Apostolate, in maintaining and promoting unity, reaches back even to the days of St. John, and thus has the Apostolic sanction, and that this idea of the Church arose in the first centuries by an inward necessity.

The later development of the doctrine of the Church, however, is steadily tending to a deeper consciousness of the importance of the Church, and more emphasis is being laid upon the confessions of the Church, and its authority as a divine institution.

Dorner, though a speculative Theologian, gives some good suggestions:

1. The Church is called *invisible*: 1) because its spiritual essence, as well as the work of the Holy Spirit generally, is not perceptible *to sense*; 2) because it cannot be known with certainty who are among the true believers; 3) but it does not mean that the *Church cannot be recognized*, for the Church has her marks (Word and Sacraments) by which we may know that she exists and where she exists.

2. The Church is called *visible*: 1) so far as the invisible Church has outward signs; for faith is assured that where Word and Sacraments are observed, there is the Church, for the means of grace are not ineffectual; 2) because believers who are members of the Church on earth are visible persons; 3) because the Church consists of believers who hold communion with those not yet believers in order to lead them to faith.

3. We can only speak of the *visibility* and *invisibility* of one and the same Church, not of a *visible* and *invisible* Church, as if there were two separate churches.

4. This distinction of the Church as visible and invisible has great value in its correct confessional statement.

   1) The value is *defensive*, and a bulwark of pure Reformation doctrine in contra-distinction to Roman Catholicism, for union with Christ through faith is the great thing necessary.

   2) The value is *critical* and *polemical*, not only with reference to Donatistic tendencies and Romanism, but also with internal reference,—for it keeps the consciousness awake

to the difference between the *essence* of the Church and its *empirical* manifestation.

3) The value is *irenical* and has a Christian ecumenical character. For if communion with Christ by faith is the chief thing, then also those in other churches, beyond the limits of the Lutheran Church, *who are in communion with Christ*, the true and living Head of the Church, are His people. "Christ is not so poor as to have His Church only in Sardinia."

The *Dogmatics* of Martensen, translated into English as early as 1866, has left its Lutheran impress on the theology of England. Though not strictly confessional, being speculative on many points, the work is always worthy of examination.

With Martensen the *formal* principle of Protestantism is "the Holy Scriptures in their indissoluble connection with the *confessing* Church." The *material* principle with him is not what is usually called *Justification by faith*, but he would use this expression to denote "subjective Christianity, the regenerated mind, the new creature in Christ, in whom the certainty of Justification through Christ, is the center of life."

When the *material* principle is neglected, and the *formal* principle is maintained in the form of *tradition*, we have one-sided Catholicism; if the *formal* principle be predominably maintained in the form of the *Scriptures*, then this gives us the legal Church, the tendency of Reformed Protestantism and of the Pietism of the seventeenth century.

When the *material* principle is maintained, and the *formal* principle sacrificed, when the individual Christian severs himself from all connection with history and tradition, and lightly esteems the written Word, relying upon his being born of the Spirit—then originate *sects*, based on visionariness and fanaticism.

"The Evangelical Church appears in two leading forms, the Lutheran and Reformed. The Swiss Reformation started primarily from the *formal* principle, that of the authority of the Scriptures; whereas the Lutheran originated more especially in the material principle, in the depths of the Christian consciousness, in an experience of sin and redemption."

"The Lutheran Reformation manifested the greatest caution to tradition, and observed the principle of rejecting nothing that could be reconciled with the Scriptures; whereas the Swiss

Reformation introduced in many respects a direct opposition between the biblical and the ecclesiastical, and in several particulars followed the principle that all ecclesiastical institutions should be rejected unless they could be deduced from the letter of the Bible."

The antithesis between the two churches cannot be designated by saying that the Lutheran Protestantism is more "emotional" and Reformed Protestantism more "intellectual," but it is better to say "that the Reformed Church, although vigorously protesting against the legal Church of Rome, is nevertheless infected with a legal spirit, whereas the germ of the fullness of the Gospel is found in Lutheranism."

In recent views of the Church it is charged that there have been some tendencies to Romanizing theories.

Stahl, the eminent jurist, Vilmar, Loehe and others laid special stress upon the Church as a divine institution with divinely appointed outward ordinances, realities distinct from the congregation and superior to it, and emphasized the ministerial office as directly instituted by God, and maintained that the office of the ministry was given to the Church as a whole.

These views were opposed by the Erlangen school (Hoefling, Harless, Von Zezschwitz, Thomasius, Harnack, Delitzsch), who emphasized the Church as the congregation of saints, and maintained that the office of the ministry rested in the congregation rather than in the Church as a whole.

These two diverse views have been the occasion of much controversy among some of the German Lutheran Synods of this country. The views in general as held by Stahl and Vilmar were favored by Grabau and his adherents (Buffalo Synod), and were especially opposed, not without a certain degree of extravagance of language on some points, by Dr. Walther and the Missouri Synod.

This controversy was the direct cause of the organization of the German Iowa Synod, for its founders were men sent over to this country by Loehe, and when these could neither adopt the views of the Buffalo Synod nor those of the Missouri Synod, they began independent work further West. The Iowa Synod takes the same position, in general, on the doctrine of the Church and of the ministry as the General Council.

CHURCH GOVERNMENT

Concerning the question of Church Government there are four leading views:

1. The *Roman Catholic* view which not only maintains the divine origin and authority of Episcopacy, but holds that all bishops are subject to the Pope of Rome as the vicar of Christ.

a) The *Eastern Church* also holds to the divine origin of the Episcopacy, to the transmission of Apostolic grace, and to Apostolic succession, but refuses to recognize the supreme Authority of the Roman Pontiff.

b) The *Jansenist* Church of Holland and the *Old Catholics* agree with the Roman Catholic Church on the question of Episcopacy, but refuse to accept the Supremacy of the Pope.

2. The High-Church Episcopal or *Anglican* theory, in essential particulars is the same as the Roman Catholic view, but it differs in this, that it denies the authority of the Pope as the vicar of Christ and infallible successor of Peter, and does not place *ordination* among the Sacraments. It regards, however, Episcopacy as indispensable to the very being of the Church, holds to the transmission of the grace of ordination, and accepts *Apostolic* succession. "Bishops, as being the successors of the Apostles are possessed of the same power of jurisdiction" (*Blunt*). "Besides the Common Faith and the Common Sacraments" they add a *third* mark of the Church, "a continuous ministry and discipline" (*Norris*). The Anglican Church "clearly asserts *her own* belief that the threefold Orders of Bishops, Priests, and Deacons, are of Apostolic origin and authority" (*Norris*).

a) Another view, known as the Low or *Broad* Church view, represented by such scholars as Lightfoot, Stanley, Alford, Hatch, and others, regard the Episcopacy as desirable and necessary for the *well* being of the Church, but not necessary for its existence. Their best writers agree that the *diocesan* Episcopate developed out of the presbyterate, and that there are only two orders of the ministry in the N.T., bishop-presbyters and deacons.

b) The *Reformed Episcopal* Church holds to an Episcopacy of expediency. She recognizes but two orders in the ministry,—the presbyterate and the diaconate. The Episcopate is not an *order*, but an office, the bishop being simply the first presbyter.

c) The *Methodist* and *Moravian* Episcopacy is merely a matter of expediency. The Moravian Church has the Apostolical succession, but lays no stress upon it. The Episcopacy of the Methodist Church is neither diocesan, nor hierarchical, but of an itinerant and missionary character. They could not lay claim to Apostolical Succession, even if they wanted to.

d) In the *Lutheran Church*, bishops are not unknown. She has them where on the whole it was thought best to have them. The Lutheran Church regards the Episcopate as *one* form of government, but not necessarily the only form. She has the Apostolic Succession even in the High Church sense in Sweden and Norway, and she could have held it everywhere had she been foolish enough to attach any importance to it. The question whether the Episcopal government is to be restored in the Lutheran Church in general and introduced into our Church in this country is purely a question of expediency for the Lutheran Church herself or any Synod to determine. It is not the Episcopate in itself, but only false views in regard to its necessity, and objectionable features in its administration, which are irreconcilable with the principles of the Lutheran Church. The necessary features, supervision, visitation, ordination, have been perpetuated in many countries in the Superintendents. Their rights are constitutionally assigned to Presidents of Conferences and synods in this country.

3. The Presbyterian Polity holds that Church government resides in the presbyters or elders, and that in the churches of the Apostolic age there were three classes of ministers or office-bearers, 1) pastors or teaching elders, 2) ruling elders, and 3)

deacons. Some Presbyterians maintain that this form of government is directly enjoined in Scripture and therefore *Jus divinum*, of divine right, while others only hold the view that it is clearly sanctioned by Scripture.

1) It was Calvin who first put into practical operation this idea of lay-eldership in Geneva (1541). In conjunction with the pastors, the lay-elders have oversight of the doctrine, life and walk of the individual believers of the congregation. The deacons serve the church in works of love, especially toward the poor, the sick, and the afflicted. Preachers, elders, and deacons, form the presbytery of the congregation, whose vocation is to build up the congregation.

2) This Presbyterian Polity has spread over all Reformed Protestantism (France, Great Britain, Germany, America), and has been adopted by many Lutheran churches, both in Germany and in this country. In fact, Presbyterianism in its generic sense, is the form of Church government most generally adopted by Lutheran Synods. The Reformed Churches believe that by this form of government they have introduced the primitive and Apostolic order, but in this they are mistaken, for the Apostolic order knew nothing of an eldership distinct from the ministry proper.

4. The fourth chief view is that no form of government was instituted by Christ or His Apostles, that there was originally no distinction between clergy and laity, but that an organization took place in due time, for the sake of order and expediency.

1) Congregationalism is an independent system of church government as fundamentally distinct from Episcopacy and Presbyterianism as they are from each other. There is some difference between the Congregationalism of England and that of this country. Both emphasize the *self-government* of local congregations, but in American Congregationalism more stress is laid on *the duty of fellowship* between sister churches. Dexter draws the following distinction between English and American Congregationalism: "Congregationalism as a system is to be conceived of, not, like Independency, as a circle all of whose parts are tied to, and evolved from a single center; but rather as an ellipse, whose two foci, of *self-completeness* and *equal fellowship*, symmetrically control its development." "The N.T. contains in express precept, or in the practice of the Apostles and primitive

churches, ail the principles of church organization and government." According to their view, *democracy* is the best species of government, and this polity is suggested by Scripture.

2) The *Baptists* in their form of government are strictly *congregational.*

3) In the Lutheran Church we also find the *congregational* form of government represented, especially in the Synodical Conference and a few Independent Synods. Where Synods have only advisory power, and no legislative power, the polity is mainly *congregational.*

Constitution of the Church in Apostolic Times

Closely connected with the doctrine of the Church is the science of Ecclesiastical Polity. We will here discuss a few points that may be of general interest. The discussion is largely based upon the writings of Dr. Krauth (whether published, as in the earlier volumes of the *Lutheran Church Review*, or in *manuscript*) and upon the standard work of Richter.

The object of Ecclesiastical Polity is to present the history and science of the administration of the Church as a visible organization—to exhibit the principles which regulate the governmental rights, duties, powers, and limitations of the Church, as a whole and of each of its parts. As the basis for further study let us briefly trace the history of the *Constitution of the Church* in *Apostolic Times*. See also 63 *above*.

1. The Apostles were missionaries and extended the Church by organizing believers into congregations.

2. An essential part of the organization of a congregation was connected with the calling of a Pastor who was to rule spiritually the congregation, conduct the public services, and administer the Sacraments.

3. A careful study of all passages in the N.T., in which the two names occur, shows that the words *Elder* (Presbyter) and *Bishop* are entirely coordinate. A N.T. bishop is an elder, and a N.T. elder is a bishop. There is no distinction among the elders. In 1 Tim. 5:17 the emphasis is not on the word *rule*, but on the word *well*. There were no *ruling* elders in contradistinction to *teaching* elders.

4. That bishops and presbyters were identical is also shown by the concurrent testimony of the Earliest Fathers.

5. Clement of Rome most explicitly teaches:

1) That ministers of the congregation are the successors of the Apostles.

2) That there were but *two orders* of workers in the congregation.

3) That the *Presbyters* and *Bishops* were absolutely co-ordinate and co-incident.

4) That there is, beside the pastorate, no ordinary office in the Church of Apostolic appointment, except that of *deacons*.

6. We thus conclude that the bishops or presbyters and the deacons are the sole officers of the N.T. Church.

7. There is no warrant whatever in N.T. history, nor in the early history of the Church, for a *jus divinum* diocesan episcopacy (by divine right), nor for a *jus divinum* lay presbyterial office (ruling elder). See 63 *above*.

Let us now take up the question of the *Diaconate*. A careful study of Acts 6:1–6 shows:

1. That the Twelve Apostles are at first the sole directors and administrators of the Church in spiritual guidance and in matters of business.

2. After the Apostleship the first office established in the Church was the diaconate.

3. The functions to which deacons were elected were functions which had been exercised by the Apostles; hence the duties of the deacon were not lay-duties, but official and ministerial in the wide sense of the word.

4. They were chosen as aids to the Apostles to take a less difficult and less important part of the work, and the true conception of the office of deacon is that he is the minister's aid.

5. The Apostles suggested the creation of the new office.

6. The persons chosen were elected by popular vote.

7. They were ordained by the Twelve with imposition of hands.

8. The Twelve now devoted themselves without interruption to prayer and the ministry of the Word.

9. The deacons had larger functions than those which would be naturally assigned them now in the Lutheran Church, on the current misconception of the nature of this office.

10. This diaconate was the same as the later diaconate men tioned in the N.T.

1) They were permanent officials in the church.

2) They were not the same as the presbyters.

3) Nor did the seven branch out into two orders, the diaconate and the presbyterate.

11. This office of the diaconate was entirely new.

1) It was not a continuation of the order of Levites.

2) Nor the adaptation of an office in the synagogue.

3) Not of the Chazan or attendant, who took care of the building and the preparation for the services of the synagogue.

12. The principal work assigned to the deacons was the relief of the poor.

13. Teaching was only incidental to their office, as in the case of Philip and Stephen.

14. All the qualifications emphasized by St. Paul (1 Tim. 3:8–13) are such as are especially necessary in going from house to house, entrusted with the distribution of alms.

15. The office spread from the Mother Church at Jerusalem into all the Churches.

16. The strict seclusion of the female sex required also a female diaconate (Rom. 16:1). The qualifications are given in 1 Tim. 3:11.17. The deacons take rank after the presbyters or bishops.

Bishops and Presbyters. See also *above.*

1. It is beyond doubt that in the N.T. *bishop* and *elder* are titles of the same office, and that consequently in the first period several *bishops* belonged to a single congregation.

2. The office of *presbyter* or *elder* takes its name and origin from the synagogue.

3. A body of elders looked after the government of the synagogue.

4. After the persecution of 44 A. D., on the dispersion of the Twelve, the same government by elders was provided for the Mother Church (Acts 11:30).

5. Paul and Barnabas appointed elders in every church founded by them (Acts 14:23).

6. The word *bishop* designates the same office, but has its origin among the Greek or Hellenic Christian Gentiles.

7. The duties of the Presbyters or Bishops were twofold:
   1. Oversight or government.
   2. Teaching. (1 Tim. 3:2; Tit. 1:9).

8. In Eph. 4:11 the expression "pastors and teachers" describes the same office under two aspects.

9. The Apostles were not bishops, for like the prophets and evangelists they held no *local* office.

10. In the N.T. we may trace two stages of the development of Church Government in the Gentile Churches:
   1. Occasional supervision by the Apostles themselves, as in the case of the offender at Corinth (1 Cor. 5:3, 4).
   2. The Apostles delegated their power to others, but not permanently, as in the case of Timothy at Ephesus (1 Tim. 1:3; 3:14; 2 Tim. 4:9, 21), and of Titus at Crete (Tit. 1:5; 3:12).
   3. We have no fuller development in the N.T. The angels of the seven churches are no exception, for these angels evidently are congregational bishops or pastors presiding over these churches.
   4. At the close of the Apostolic age there was no trace of the *diocesan* Episcopate.

The Development of the Episcopal Hierarchy

The development of the *diocesan* Episcopate was gradual, and as follows: The Presbyter-bishop, and several bishops belonged to a single congregation. Then, even as early as 100 A. D. (in the writings of Ignatius), the *one* bishop in each congregation, with presbyters and deacons, known as the Congregational Episcopate, a development out of the presbyterate. From this point the Church in her liberty developed the *diocesan* Episcopacy. The development of the Episcopacy is connected with three great names, Ignatius, Irenæus and Cyprian.

The desire of unity led the Church to the holding of *Synods.* The first Synod or Council has its minutes recorded in Acts 15:1– 30, and we may notice the following facts: The deliberations were confined to the Apostles and elders (Acts 15:6, 12). The discussion took place in the presence of the multitude (Acts 15:12). The whole church or congregation united in the reception of Paul and Barnabas (Acts 15:4), and united in the election of men to accompany them in their return to Antioch (Acts 15:22), but the people apparently took no part officially in the discussion of the Council (Acts 15:12). Synods were found so useful that, in the second century, special synods were held to settle questions of doctrine and usage, and synods soon began to be fixed institutions, as in Greece. In the third century synods appeared in North Africa and Cappadocia as essential elements of Church constitution.

The history of the early Councils shows:

1) That the presbyters originally participated in these Synods, in connection with the bishops.

2) The assent of the people was asked on the question discussed.

3) As the idea that the Holy Spirit wrought through the diocesan episcopate took deeper root, the participation of the people and the rights of the presbyters fell into the background.

4) The bishops soon ceased to regard themselves as the representatives of their congregations, and now began to act as if endowed with independent authority. Claiming the cooperation of the Holy Sprit, they laid down their decisions as law (Greek *kanon,* rule, hence canon, *canonical law*).

5) The circles out of which the Synods were originally convened, were the provinces, which had the bond of a common nationality and a common language—hence provincial and national councils.

6) Not until Constantine the Great (306–337 A. D.) gave political recognition to the Church, and the inhabited world was regarded as coincident with the Roman Empire, did any Synod claim the name of Œcumenical or Universal.

The eight earliest Ecumenical Councils are:

1) I. Nice, 325 A. D.; 2) I. Constantinople, 381 A. D.; 3) Ephesus, 431 A. D.; 4) Calcedon, 451 A. D.; 5) II. Constantinople, 553 A. D.; 6) III. Constantinople, 680 A. D.; 7) II. Nice, 787 A. D.; 8) IV. Constantinople, 869, A. D.

The rise of regularly organized Synods led to the development of the *Metropolitan Constitution*. The life of the Church within a province soon formed its central point in the Bishops of the great leading cities, the *Metropolitan* centers. The metropolitan bishops consequently were looked upon as best able to secure the unity of the Church administration within a province. The Council of Nice considers the metropolitan constitution as already an existent thing, and assigns a certain prominence, on metropolitan grounds, to the bishops of Alexandria, Antioch and Rome.

The steps which led to the *Roman hierarchical* form of government can be traced as follows:

1) Congregational episcopacy, *Jus divinum* (by divine right); 2) Diocesan episcopacy, *Jus divinum;* 3) Metropolitan episcopacy, *Jus divinum*; 4) the Supremacy of the Pope, *Jus divinum.*

The relation of the Church to the Civil Orders.

The character of Christianity enabled it readily to assimilate itself with the order of the State. Its first triumph, in a political aspect, was its being put upon a common ground of protection with other forms of religion by Constantine the Great. From the time of the union between the Church and State, the spurious "Catholic" Church developed elements which led to the theory of the primacy of the Church of Rome, and to the claim of the Pope to universal dominion.

Church Polity of the Roman Catholic Church during the Middle Ages.

The Pope began to be regarded as the Supreme authority in Christendom, holding the right of deciding the great questions of State as well as of the Church. The Episcopate was stripped of many of its highest prerogatives. When the Papacy reached its height of power strong evidences of a great reactionary tendency made themselves felt. The Council of Pisa (1409) declared that supreme authority lay in a General Council, not in the Pope; the Council of Constance (1414–1418) claimed such a supreme authority; and the Council of Basle (1431–1443) deposed the Pope and limited the Papal power.

The Ecclesiastical Polity of the Reformation Period

The Reformation and the Polity of the Church.
The doctrine of the Reformation most powerfully influenced the government of the Church. Luther soon discovered that the Christian Church and the Roman Church are not identical. He soon saw that the N.T. makes no such distinction between the clergy and laity as was taught and practiced by the Roman Church. In place of a priesthood communicating salvation, the Reformation laid down as a postulate, the universal priesthood of all believers.

The N.T. Church does not know of any sacerdotal or priestly system. The ministry is not identical with, nor derived from, the Levitical priesthood, and is not designated to offer sacrifice and to make atonement. The privileges of the universal priesthood are never transferred to the ministry.

The Reformation introduced a new order of divine service, and established the office of the evangelical ministry. In the judgment of the Reformers the great significance of the ministry is, that in it the universal priestly calling of all believers comes into a rightly ordered exercise. With this idea of the ministry began the renewed constitution of the Church. The place in which the pastor is to work is the congregation by which he has been called.

He is to preach the gospel and administer the sacraments. His office is representative, not vicarial. His acts are not his own but the acts of the congregation.

In the spirit of this conception of the ministerial office the German cities and states began to arrange their constitutions. The disturbed condition of society and the various necessities of the Church led to the establishing of a stricter government, and to a disposition to appeal to the State for protection, which later under the development of the territorial system led to such disastrous results. In the larger cities at the head of the clergy was the Superintendent, who with the other clergy form the Ministerium, which decides all matters relating to the Word of God and exercises Church discipline.

Further unfolding of the Church Constitution during the 16th Century.

The faith of the Protestant Evangelical Church, *i.e.*, the Lutheran Church, embodied itself in the Confessions as published in 1580 under the title of "The Book of Concord." The importance of the Lutheran Confessions for Church law is not so much that they attempt to present the complete system of an unchangeable constitution; But they unfold on the basis of Scripture only the most important principles, which will develop themselves in a manifold way in the practical life of the Church. Of special importance are the affirmations in regard to the limitation of Church power and the position of the ministry. The foundation of Lutheran Church Polity is specifically laid in Art. XXVIII. of the Augsburg Confession.

The outline of Art. XXVIII. of A. C, *Of Ecclesiastical Power* is as follows:

1) The importance of the doctrine (§ 1–4).

2) The Scriptural doctrine stated (§ 5–12).

1. The power of the keys (ecclesiastical power), according to the Gospel, is a power or command of God to preach the Gospel, to remit and retain sins, and to administer the Sacraments (John 20:21–23; Mark 16:15, 16) (§ 5–7).

2. This power is put into execution only by teaching or preaching God's Word and administering the sacraments, in accordance with the call. (§ 8–10).

3. As ecclesiastical power is concerning things eternal, and is exercised only by the ministry of the word, it does not hinder the political government, any more than the art of singing hinders the political government (§ 11, 12).

3) There is a distinction between the ecclesiastical and civil powers (§ 13–18).

1. Our teachers distinguish between the duties of each power, one from the other, and warn all men to honor both powers, and to acknowledge both to be the highest gift and blessing of God.

4) Limitations to the Jurisdiction of bishops (§ 19–29).

1. Bishops may exercise two forms of jurisdiction, civil and ecclesiastical (§ 19).

2. We must distinguish between the two (§ 20).

3. The ecclesiastical jurisdiction belongs to bishops, by divine right, only as ministers of the Word, and the only jurisdiction they have is that of the Word and Sacraments, to remit and to retain sins, to judge doctrine and to exercise discipline (§ 21).

4. In the exercise of this office the Churches owe them obedience necessarily and of divine right, Luke 10:16 (§ 22).

5. If they teach or determine anything contrary to the Gospel, then the Churches have a command of God which prohibits obedience, Matt. 7:15; Gal. 1:8, 9; 2 Cor. 13:8, 10. (§ 23–28).

6. All other powers, like matrimony, etc., they have only by human right (§ 29).

5) Their power to institute ceremonies in the Church examined (§ 30–68).

1. The argument stated by which they claim power to make laws concerning holidays and orders of ministers (§ 30–33).

2. They have no power to ordain anything contrary to the Gospel, nor to require the observation of any traditions to merit grace or righteousness (§ 34–38).

3. By imposing such traditions and laws they ensnare men's consciences (§ 39–42).

4. The making of such laws and traditions to merit grace strictly prohibited in Scripture, Col. 2:16, 20–23; Tit. 1:14; Matt. 15:14; 1 Tim. 4:1 (§ 43–49).

5. It is contrary to the doctrine of Christian liberty for any bishops to institute such human ordinances, Gal. 5:1 (§ 50–52).

6. It is lawful for the ministry (bishops or pastors) to make ordinances for the sake of order in the Church, but not that we may merit grace (§ 53, 54).

7. Such ordinances it behooves the Churches to keep for the sake of order (1 Cor. 14:40; Phil. 2:14), but they do not account them as things necessary to salvation (§ 55–64).

8. And such traditions and rites change and grow out of use as time passes by (§ 65–68).

6) An appeal to the bishops to suffer the Gospel to be purely taught, and to relax such ordinances and traditions which cannot be observed without sin (§ 69–77).

Outline of the Apology on Art. XIV., Of Ecclesiastical Orders.

1. Concerning Church Government, the Confessors teach that no man should publicly teach in the Church or administer the Sacraments, *unless he be rightly called* (§ 24 *a*).

2. It is their greatest wish to maintain Church Polity and the grades in the Church, even though they have been made by human authority (§ 24 *b*).

3. For Church discipline was instituted by the Fathers as laid down in the ancient canons, with a good and useful intention (§ 24 c).

4. The cruelty of the bishops is the reason why canonical government is in some cases dissolved (§ 25–27).

5. We would gladly maintain ecclesiastical order, but the unrighteous cruelty of the bishops prevents us (§ 28).

Outline of the Apology on Art. XV., Of Human Traditions in the Church.

1. Such *ecclesiastical rites* are to be observed as can be observed without sin and are profitable for tranquility and good order in the Church (§ 1 *a*).

2. But such human traditions cannot merit grace, nor make satisfaction for sins (§ 1 *b*, 2).

3. The adversaries in teaching otherwise are openly Judaizing (§ 3–5).

4. Scripture clearly teaches that human observances do not merit the remission of sins, and that Christ is our only Mediator (§ 6–12).

5. Human rites were instituted by the Fathers for the sake of good order in the Church (§ 13).

6. The folly of thinking that human rites justify or are profitable for meriting grace (§ 14–17).

7. The doctrine of the adversaries is "the very form and constitution of the Kingdom of Antichrist" (§ 18–21).

8. Traditions have "a show of wisdom" (Col. 2:23), but are easily perverted (§ 22–24).

9. Infinite evil results follow such perversions (§ 25–28).

10. Such human traditions are not necessary for justification (§ 29, 30).

11. And the bishops have no power to institute services with this design (§31–37).

12. All useful ordinances, godly ceremonies, good Church customs (the observance of Sunday, of the three great Festivals, Christmas, Easter, Pentecost; the weekly celebration of the Lord's Supper; singing of Psalms; catechisation, etc.) and Church discipline, should be maintained (§ 38–44).

13. True discipline of the body also ought not to be neglected (§ 45–48).

14. The true solution of all these difficulties lies in the true use of Christian liberty (§ 49–52).

Outline of the Apology on Art. XXVIII., Of Ecclesiastical Power.
1. The points at issue in this controversy with Rome (§ 1–6).

1) The adversaries do not care that the churches be rightly taught and the sacraments rightly administered (§ 1–3).

2) They demand that human traditions be observed more accurately than the Gospel (§ 4, 5).

3) The bishops maintain they have the power of rule and of coercive correction, and have authority to frame laws, contrary to the Gospel, useful for obtaining eternal life (§ 6).

2. The bishops have no right to impose traditions upon the Church in addition to the Gospel to merit remission of sins and righteousness (§ 7–14).

1) For it is only for Christ's sake, by faith, that we freely receive remission of sins (§ 7).

2) For human traditions are useless services, as hearts are only purified by faith, Acts 15:8–11 (§ 8).

3) Traditions do not conduce to eternal life (§ 9, 10).

4) The only power a true bishop has as a minister of the Gospel is *a) the power of the order,* i.e., the ministry of the Word and Sacraments, and *b) the power of Jurisdiction,* i.e., the authority to excommunicate the guilty, and to absolve those who are converted and seek absolution (§ 11–13).

5) Even this power is not tyrannical, *i.e.,* without law; nor regal, *i.e.,* above law; but according to rule and order, for they

have a fixed command and a fixed Word of God how to teach and to exercise jurisdiction (§ 14 *a*).

6) Though they have some jurisdiction, it does not follow that they are able to institute new services contrary to the Gospel (§ 14 *b*).

3. Traditions may be observed when not regarded necessary services (§ 15, 16).

1) Bishops may establish ordinances for the sake of order and tranquility in the Church (§ 15).

2) But the use of such ordinances must be left free, and it must be clearly understood that they are liable to change with time (§ 16).

4. The arguments of the adversaries answered (§ 17–27).

1) They cannot quote Luke 10:16 in their favor, for this has no reference to their traditions, but is most effective against traditions. Christ wishes His own Word to be heard, not human traditions (§ 17–19).

2) Nor Heb. 13:17, for this does not establish a rule of the bishops apart from the Gospel, but requires *obedience to the Gospel* (§ 20).

3) Nor Matt. 23:3, for this does not mean that we should do anything contrary to God's command and Word. "We must obey God rather than men", Acts 5:29 (§ 21).

4) The doctrine of our Confession does not cause public scandal. All we seek is the truth, and we dare not desert it (§ 22–27).

Teaching of the Smalcald Articles (Luther), Art-VII., Of the Keys.

1. "The keys are an office and power given by Christ to the Church for binding and loosing sins."

119. Art. IX., *Of Excommunication.*

1. The greater excommunication as the Pope calls it, is a civil penalty, and does not pertain to us ministers of the Church.

2. We here refer to true Christian excommunication, when ministers "prohibit manifest and obstinate sinners from the

sacrament and other communion of the Church until they are reformed and avoid sin".

Outline of Appendix to the Smalcald Articles, Part II., Of the Power and Jurisdiction of Bishops.

1. All ministers of the Gospel, *by divine right,* have the same ecclesiastical power (§ 60–64).

1) They equally have *the power of the order, i.e.,* to preach the Gospel and administer the sacraments (§ 60 *a*).

2) They equally have *the power of jurisdiction,* to excommunicate and to absolve (§ 60 *b*).

3) Whether they be called pastors, or elders, or bishops (§ 61, 62).

4) By *human authority* a distinction may and has been drawn between bishops and pastors (§ 63, 64).

2. The Church always has the right to elect, call and ordain ministers (§ 65–72.)

1) For as the grades of bishop and pastor, by divine right, are not diverse, any pastor (not necessarily a bishop) may ordain certain suitable persons to the ministry (§ 65).

2) So when the regular bishops refuse to administer ordination, the churches retain their right (§ 66).

3) This authority to call, elect and ordain ministers is a gift exclusively given to the Church, which no human power can wrest from the Church (§ 67).

4) The keys have been given to the Church, and not merely to certain persons (§ 68, 69).

5) Therefore, if the bishops will not ordain suitable persons, the Church is in duty bound to elect and ordain ministers (§ 70–72).

3. As bishops have so basely abused *the power of jurisdiction* (of excommunication and absolution), it is right also to restore this power to pastors, to whom, by Christ's command, it belongs (§ 73–76).

4. As the bishops in many cases (matrimony, etc.,) have jurisdiction only by human right, on account of their unjust laws (prohibition of marriage between sponsors, forbidding an

innocent party to marry after divorce, celibacy of priests, etc.,) such jurisdiction ought to be withdrawn (§ 77, 78).

5. These reasons are sufficient why the bishops should no longer be recognized (§ 79).

6. And in addition to all this, the bishops are defrauding the Church by misusing the alms of the Church for their own luxury (§ 80–82).

Luther's Teaching on Ecclesiastical Government. (See Koestlin.)

1. In connection with his controversy with the Zwickau Prophets, and in a communication addressed to the "Council and People of Prague", Luther took occasion to develop more fully the doctrine of the *universal priesthood* of all believers (1523 A. D.).

1) All offices in the Church must be conferred by fellow-members or the congregation.

2) Whoever wishes to exercise the office of *the ministry* must have a regular and formal call.

3) To be a priest, exercising the universal priesthood, is not the same as to be a minister; all believers are priests, but ministers are called and made.

4) A Christian congregation (or Church) has the right to call ministers.

5) To exercise the office of the ministry publicly and habitually is not permitted except with the consent of the whole body, or the Church; in case of necessity, it is different.

6) He advises the *Council* of Prague, as representatives of the Church, to elect pastors, to ordain them, and commend them to the people.

7) Bishops are not to appoint any pastors, however, "without the will, election and call of the congregation."

8) In case of necessity—for this knows no law—a preacher may be secured, either by pleading for one or by appointment by the secular authorities; or an individual believer, if he has the abilities, may arise and teach and assume the office.

9) But Luther, already as early as 1523, emphasized the fact that the individual believer should employ his authority as a member of the universal priesthood only *in case of necessity.*

10) But this doctrine was soon perverted by many to the grossest abuse.

11) In opposition to the Anabaptists, Luther expounds the doctrine of the Call to the Ministry still more emphatically, and warns the Churches against these self-appointed preachers who "come of their own choice and piety," and most positively insists upon the exclusive authority of every pastor in his own parish.

12) He now no longer leaves any room for the free exercise of public preaching.

13) And the community of believers falls for him into two sections, preachers and the laity, and though in his later period Luther felt himself called upon to emphasize more fully the authority and dignity of the ministerial office, nevertheless the main features of the doctrine remained unchanged.

Summary of Luther's later Teaching.

1) The universal priesthood belongs to all believers, and includes the right and authority to teach the Word of God.

2) The power of the keys belongs to the whole Church and to all members, and we may even say, the preaching office belongs to all.

3) But not all can preach, but one must speak for the congregation.

4) The office of the ministry must be committed to one person.

5) Clerical rank is a ministry and calling of the ministers of the Church.

6) Those who have been elected and called, if they have suitable gifts, shall be ordained.

7) The pastors or bishops already in office shall participate in the induction of every new candidate into the ministry, approve of his doctrine, and confirm his appointment by the laying on of hands.

8) As a minister he is the *public administrant* of that which belongs to the entire congregation, appointed by the congregation, and called and ordained of God.

9) He exercises spiritual authority publicly and officially, through the *power of the order* (the Word and Sacraments), and through *the power of jurisdiction* (spiritual loosing and binding).

10) He rules by means of the Word, and is a bishop or overseer, a watchman, and his power a ministry.

Luther is consistent and harmonious in his teaching, though we can trace a development in the clearness and fullness of his statement.

1) Many find a seeming conflict on this subject between the private writings of Luther and the conservative statements of the Confessions.

2) Others, holding most diverse views on the subject of the Church and Church Polity, with equal confidence and assurance quote Luther as co-inciding with their special theory.

3) In Luther's case pre-eminently, as in the case with all writers who have written extensively, and have often been obliged to write hurriedly, we must not forget to interpret and modify one statement by all the others, and carefully note the occasion and the time when written.

4) The intensity of Luther's conviction and the singleness of his aim often led him to a certain isolation of statement, so that what seems to be asserted absolutely, we find from other passages of his writings, must be taken relatively.

The Teaching of Melanchthon.

Melanchthon emphasizes the fact that congregations should have a voice in the calling of pastors, and have the right of rejecting ungodly or unsuitable men. So in the administration of discipline, he maintains that it is not lawful for the pastor alone to pronounce sentence of excommunication, but the judgment of some of the more honorable men of the Church should be employed. But by the close of the 16th century there was allowed only a sort of negative co-operation to the members of a parish in the appointment of a pastor.

The Doctrine of Ecclesiastical Polity in its Later Development.

At the end of the 16th century the constitution of the Lutheran Church had found its highest point in the princes, and its administrative organs in the consistories. With these stood the body of the ministry, not indeed as an organized force, yet presenting important limitations. Under both, without taking part in political rule or in ecclesiastical administration, was the mass of the unofficial laity.

The theologians now taught the doctrine of the Three Estates:

1) The Political Estate, the Rights of the State.
2) The Ecclesiastical Estate, or the Rights of the Church.
3) The Domestic Estate, or the Rights of the Family.

This doctrine of the three Estates, known as the Episcopal System, was modified in various respects.

The different rights then came to be divided as follows:

1) The clergy exercised *material* Church power, *i.e.*, controlled the judgment of doctrine and the administration of discipline.

2) The princes exercised the *formal* power, *i.e.*, they gave external sanction to that which was offered them by the clergy.

3) To the people belonged the right to accept and use what was given them, and to obey what was commanded.

This theory was developed by the theologian Carpzov, whose object, by extending the rights of the clergy, was to preserve purity of doctrine. It made the prince or ruler *summits episcopus,* combining in his person the highest spiritual with the highest civil authority.

Pietism in emphasizing the universal priesthood sought to cure the languishing Church, and indirectly was the means of introducing the *Territorial System.*

This was developed under the influence of Thomasius (*d.* 1728) in direct personal opposition to Carpzov. It assumed that the prince or ruler as sovereign ruler in the State possessed the highest ecclesiastical authority. The headship of the Church thus became an inherent element of civil government. It denies that the Church is a special order of life, with a government of its own, working by ecclesiastical means.

Under the influence of Pietism the third view, known as the *Collegial System* now rose to prominence. The greatest early representative of this view is Pfaff (*d.* 1760). The third Estate, the people, was now brought more prominently into view. According to the Collegial System the exercise of Church power on the part of the Sovereign or Magistracy derived its right only from the consent of the Church, and all matters pertaining to doctrine, worship, ecclesiastical law and its administration, installation of clergy, and excommunication, belong to the whole Church, consisting of clergy and laity. The last struggle in the Lutheran Church in Europe may be said to lie between the Territorial and Collegiate Systems.

The Relation of the Lutheran Church to the State:
The Lutheran Church in the course of her development has stood in the closest connection with the life of the State. In consequence the government of the Church has been largely secularized. This has led to many attempts to separate Church and State, or at least to lift the Church above all the fluctuations of political life. For the most part in Europe the best solutions have been Church courts with a collegial constitution, under the control of the supreme officials of the State. The questions of Church Government in the Lutheran Church are still in course of agitation.

STUDIES IN LUTHERAN CHURCH POLITY

Introduction.

Church Polity is of vital importance and of peculiar value at the present time, on account of the great extravagance of hierarchical pretensions on the one hand, and the disorganizing laxity of sectarianism on the other. We have infallibility claimed by the Pope and virtual infallibility claimed for the people of a congregation.

Though the Lutheran Church has clearly stated the general principles underlying Church Government, yet compared with the rich maturity and perfection of her system of doctrine, her Church Polity may be regarded as relatively undeveloped. In no period of her history has there been less comprehension of her true principle of government than seems to characterize many parts of our Church in this country.

The main reason of this lies in the fact that her various nationalities, originally coming from different lands, brought with them different modes of government or no mode at all, and in the mingling of her peoples and the immense missionary activity of the churches, very little attention could be given to this problem.

But considering the great future in store for our Church in this land, it behooves us to ponder what should be the outward form of bodily organization through which the spirit of the Lutheran Church can best accomplish her great task.

The constitution or polity of the Lutheran Church may in its particular form be largely influenced by the individuality of character pertaining to particular nationalities and particular eras. Any polity must be considered as in general conformity with the will of Christ, so long as within it pure faith and Christian life can be unfolded in freedom and peace. It is on this principle that the fact is accounted for and justified that the Lutheran Church in the particular national churches has developed a Polity with more or less special peculiarities of form.

This explains why in some parts of the Lutheran Church the Episcopal form of government has been adopted, as in Norway and Sweden, while in others, as in Germany, the churches were governed by consistories constituted by the heads of government, or as later by Superintendents (Inspectors, Provosts, Deans, Seniors), while in the United States two tendencies have developed themselves, the first leaning towards the presbyterial and Synodal polity, and the second towards a congregational polity.

These diverse forms of polity do not imply that there is not some polity which is peculiarly adapted to the genius and spirit of the Lutheran Church, but it only emphasizes the fact that the Church in her relations to the State and society, in her freedom and development of the religious life, has not come to a living realization of the form of polity which is best adapted for her growth and development.

That Church Polity ought to be encouraged, in the freedom of the Church, which best solves the great problems which lie before us as a Lutheran Church in this country.

1) To develop the life and energy of the congregation without engendering a false independency.

2) To produce the highest activity in the separate congregations. The congregation is not a mere passive element; it should take an active part in the ordering of its own secular interests, and in the exercise of discipline, either directly or through its authorized representatives; in fact the welfare of the congregation depends on a healthy harmony between the activity of the pastorate and the activity of the congregation.

3) To conjoin with that activity a thorough organization which will in the highest degree promote the most perfect united action of the whole Church, and develop *living churches* in a compact and *living Church*. For it is desirable that the congregations should stand in *organic* relation with each other, as mutual aids in the conservation of pure doctrine, the ordering of divine service, the administration of discipline, and the general

development of the kingdom of God (Education, Inner Mission, Home Missions, Foreign Missions).

To the attempt to bring about the activity of the congregation we owe the congregational constitutions of recent periods, and in this effort many of our Synods in this country have been engaged. In all rightly organized congregations the pastor forms, by virtue of his office, the highest of the governing authorities.

In association with him as aids (deacons) are such persons only as are in full communion with the Church, regular in attendance in her worship, doing honor to the Word and Sacrament, and leading a life which gives credible evidence of Christian character.

The best view of the relation of the pastor to his flock is that the congregation is but an organ of the Church as a whole in placing him in its pastorate—that the minister is the minister of Christ, therefore of His whole Church, whose functions are restricted by the Church to the congregation. As an ambassador, though confined to one locality, he is yet the representative of the whole Church, for which those who made the call and the appointment are acting.

The disposition to give to the individual congregation the right to make regulations touching the general confession and the general order of the Church has arisen from a complete confusion of ideas which are partly the result of reaction against the continued neglect of the congregational element. Such a tendency unarrested runs out at last into complete independency and general anarchy. Congregations may indeed by the common constitution under which they act, make provision in certain reserved cases for special action of their own, but it is in conflict with the entire conception of representative government, that the same organic bodies which reach results in common, should have the power of overthrowing them by separate action.

Annotations on the Principles of Church Polity adopted by the
General Council

Further elucidation of this Topic. (Based on Krauth.)

As there seems to be such mistaken notions, in these unchurchly times, about the authority and power of the Church, it may be of aid to us to examine this topic more closely. The presentation will follow the order of the *Fundamental Principles of Ecclesiastical Power and Church Government* adopted by the *General Council* of the Evangelical Lutheran Church in North America, at Fort Wayne, Ind., in 1867, which is also a part of the Constitution of "The Theological Seminary of the Evangelical Lutheran Church, at Chicago, ILL."

"I. All power of the Church belongs primarily, properly and exclusively to our Lord Jesus Christ, 'true God, begotten of the Father from eternity, and true man, born of the Virgin Mary,' Mediator between God and men, and Supreme Head of the Church. This supreme and direct power is not delegated to any man or body of men upon earth."

1) This *Supreme* power has not been committed to pope, nor body of bishops, nor clergy, nor Synod, nor General Council, nor to the whole Church on earth and in heaven.

2) Still less is this power delegated to a single congregation or its pastor.

3) Christ's will and Word are supreme and the rule by them in its *direct* form is transferred to no other hands.

4) But a *subordinate* as distinguished from a *supreme* power, a *mediate* as distinguished from a *direct* power, is committed or delegated by and under Christ to the *Church* on earth.

"II. All just power exercised by the Church has been committed to her for the furtherance of the Gospel, through the Word and Sacraments, is conditioned by this end, and is derivative and pertains to her as the servant of Jesus Christ."

"The Church, therefore, has no power to bind the conscience, except as she truly teaches what her Lord teaches, and faithfully commands what He has charged her to command."

1) This implies that there is a Church on earth, and that she has functions and powers entrusted to her.

2) This implies that the Church in fact has an authority and exercises power.

3) All the well-established parts of the Church exercise well-defined powers. The exercise of some power is the necessary condition of existence.

4) When we speak of *just* power we imply that there is an *unjust* power sometimes exercised, *e.g.*, in the Church of Rome.

5) Unjust Church power may have one or more of the following features:

a) It may be disallowed of Christ and of His Word;

b) It may be monarchical, having one head upon earth;

c) It may be falsely aristocratic, in conflict with the will and right of the people, as in the Episcopal Church, when the Bishops claim power "by divine right."

6) Over against this is *just* power, characterized by its derivation from right sources, its having right ends and proper conditions.

7) The *just* power exercised by the Church involves three things:

a) That it shall concern things right in themselves;

b) That they shall be things which rightly belong to her;

c) That she shall exercise only moral and spiritual force.

For the great end of Church authority is the furtherance of the Gospel.

8) The instruments through which she is to carry out this great end are the Word and Sacraments. All her power is to be alternately exercised through these. The Church may reprove, warn, and correct through the Word, and may withhold the Sacraments from those who resist the truth.

9) This power of the Church is mainly exercised through the ministry to whom it has been committed by the Church. Baier: "The ministry of the Church bears with it the power and office, 1) of teaching publicly and administering the Sacraments according to order; and 2) the power and function of remitting and retaining Sins." The former is termed *the power of the order*; the latter, *the power of the Keys*, or the power of Jurisdiction. This power of the Keys is two-fold, loosing and binding, Matt. 16:19; John 20:23.

"III. The absolute directory of the Will of Christ is the Word of God, the Canonical Scriptures, interpreted in accordance with the 'mind of the Spirit,' by which Scriptures the Church is to be guided in every decision. She may set forth no article of faith which is not taught by the very letter of God's Word, or derived by just and necessary inference from it, and her liberty concerns those things only which are left free by the letter and spirit of God's Word."

"IV. The primary bodies through which the power is normally exercised, which Christ commits derivatively and ministerially to His Church on earth, are the Congregations. The Congregation, in the normal state, is neither the Pastor without the People, nor the People without the Pastor."

1) This implies that the exercise of Church-power on earth is a corporate one.

2) There is no ordinary Church-power on earth except the derivative and ministerial, and that power is never normally conferred on one individual, or exercised by him as an individual, that is, apart from the representative principle.

3) There is a difference between an abnormal and a normal exercise of power. Abnormal power may be exercised *a*) by an extraordinary commission from the Head of the Church, as in the case of St. Paul; *b*) under circumstances so extraordinary as to create a necessity, which transcends all ordinary rule; or, *c*) without the justification of the necessity, yet with a tacit consent of the Church.

4) Apart from abnormal cases, the ordinary corporation through which the power is finally mediated is the Church or distinct religious community, embracing pastor (or pastors) and people, in the primary organization known as a congregation.

5) To the true idea of a Christian congregation in its completeness is essential the concurrence of both pastor and people.

6) Among the various false theories of Church-power may be enumerated the following: *a*) the Papal system; *b)* the *Jus divinum* Episcopal system; *c*) the *Jus divinum* presbyterial system; *d*) the *Jus divinum,* congregational system, when it is identical with the system of independency and considers the people apart from the pastor as the total congregation.

"V. In Congregations exists the right of representation. In addition to the Pastor, who by their voluntary election is already *ex-officio* their representative, the people have the right to choose representatives from their own number to act for them, under such constitutional limitations as the Congregation approves."

1) A representative is one empowered by a principal to act for him under certain defined conditions.

2) The principle of representation meets us everywhere as one of the first necessities of social, civil and ecclesiastical activity.

3) The act of the representative, in so far as power is given to him, binds the principal; and if discretionary power is given him, and the representative acts within its limits, he binds the principal.

4) In the higher forms of human need the principle of representation becomes more and more necessary.

5) A congregation can be ruled in no way but *representatively,*—even a congregational meeting so-called, the nearest approach to a pure direct democracy, is representative. It never embraces the whole congregation—the adults represent the infant members, men represent families, and even if women vote, not all are present, the sick and the aged are absent, and unless we concede the *representative* principle, no congregational meeting would have validity, unless every member were present, and every member voted in the same way—for a majority after all represents the minority or the whole congregation.

6) If it were not for this principle of representation many congregations could never unite into general bodies.

7) Representatives act for their principals in listening, judging and deciding, under such authority as has been granted them, but that is not a representative system, which makes *the congregations in their separation* superior to the body of their own representation.

8) God calls men into the ministry by means of His Church, through which He exercises His power of appointing public teachers of the Word. No one should preach publicly and ordinarily, or administer the Sacraments, unless he be rightly and legitimately called with the ordinary calling. The power to call is a divinely given right that belongs to the whole Church, to both people and ministers, each estate virtually possessing the power of veto on the act of the other, and every call requiring the concurrence of both people and clergy.

9) When a congregation without a pastor, calls a minister as its pastor, he by this call becomes their representative in the public functions of the universal priesthood. All N.T. believers are priests and can draw near to God and offer spiritual sacrifices

through Jesus Christ, and this *universal* priesthood is common to all believers, but this universal priesthood does not confer the right to offer prayer or preach publicly representatively for all. Hence the necessity arises that some one should act representatively for all, inasmuch as the right of such a person is not individual but organic, and can be exercised only by the representation of an organism.

10) The pastor of a congregation thus becomes representative, not by the transfer of a number of individual rights, as individual, to him, but by the vocation of the whole congregation as an organism. Just as our representative system in the government of our country necessarily results from the sovereignty of the people. When each one is equally sovereign there can be no government, except in the representative principle, by which the common right invests itself in the ruler. When each man is equally president, no man is president, for presidency involves superiority; there can be no president in fact as one superior to the common level, except by the act of the many in organic unity.

11) As every minister has been called by the whole Church, and ordained by the authority of the Church, the pastor of every congregation is not only *ex-officio* a representative of the congregation, but as such is also a representative of the whole Church.

12) The system of lay-delegation did not exist in the N.T. Church, nor in the Early Church, nor is it essential to the being of the Church, however much we may regard it of value to the Church's well-being.

13) Ruling Elders, as lay-officers, are not authorized by the N.T., and were not known until the sixteenth century.

14) *Jus divinum* lay-eldership has as little support in the New Testament as *Jus divinum* Episcopacy.

15) The deacons of the Early Church were not lay-representatives of the congregation, but were ministers' aids.

16) It is only on the broad general principles of common right that congregations derive the power of representing themselves; the *Jus divinum* of congregational representation is purely generic, not scriptural.

"VI. The representatives of congregations thus convened in Synod, and acting in accordance with those conditions of mutual congregational compact, which are called a Constitution, are for the ends, and with the limitations defined in it, representatively, the Congregations themselves."

"A free, Scriptural General Council or Synod, chosen by the Church, is, within the metes and bounds fixed by the Church which chooses it, representatively that Church itself; and in this case is applicable the language of the Appendix to the Smalcald Articles, 'The judgments of Synods are the judgments of the Church.'"

1) Synodical authority is derived from the congregations; the Synod is a congregation of congregations, and what each congregation has separately, the whole of the congregations embodied through their representatives has by a stronger reason (*a fortiori*). A congregation of individuals has not the same authority as a congregation of congregations. It is as preposterous to claim that it has, as it is to say that the primary meetings of the people have more authority than the Congress of the United States, though that Congress, in a certain sense, grows out of the primary meetings.

2) The congregations, because they are the primary sources of the church-power, are thereby constituted, not the highest but the lowest church authority in all questions not strictly congregational.

3) The constitution here spoken of is a compact or solemn agreement as to the terms on which congregations will allow other congregations to take part in determining questions of common interest.

4) When congregations make such a compact and define how far the representation of the delegates shall go, they are bound up to that point by the actions of their delegates, who are indeed so far the congregation itself in each case.

5) That a free, General Council or Synod, chosen by the Church, is representatively the Church itself, arises necessarily from the representative principle. That principle holds good so long as it is possible to have representation. Whether we be represented by a direct representation or by the representation of representatives, the representation is no less real nor less derived from the primary authority, which after any number of stages is still the authority embraced in the final representation. Our people choose electors to choose a President. It is not the electors

as private men but as representatives who choose, and the choice of the electors is the choice of the people.

6) Such a representative Council or Synod must be *free*, removed from all fear of civil or ecclesiastical penalties, and from all illicit influence.

7) It must be Scriptural, resting on God's Word as the rule of faith.

8) It must be really chosen by those whom it represents.

9) It must do what it has been constituted to do.

10) Accepting these principles, so far discussed, and reasoning from them, we reach the following conclusions:

1. The Church is justly regarded by our divines as either *Synthetic* (or *Collective*) on the one hand, or *Representative* on the other.

2. A Church *synthetically* (or collectively) considered is the whole body of pastors and members, both baptized infants and adults, united in the communion of the same faith.

3. The Church *representatively* considered consists of the pastors and such other persons who represent the Church in the examination and decision of questions of doctrine and discipline.

4. The power of representing herself or of embodying herself representatively is an inherent, necessary and inalienable right of the Church.

"VII. The congregations representatively constituting the various district Synods may elect delegates through those Synods, to represent themselves in a more general body, all decisions of which, when made in conformity with the solemn compact of the Constitution, bind, so far as the terms of mutual agreement make them binding, those congregations which consent, and continue to consent, to be represented in that general body."

1) Representation is limited only by the power of actual exercise, *i.e.*, as long as we *can* represent ourselves we *may* represent ourselves.

2) Constitutions are designed for the benefit of all, but especially of minorities, because majorities can take care of themselves relatively better than minorities.

3) To say that the constitutional decisions of a body fairly representative bind those who are represented in it, is only to say that we are bound by compact and agreement.

"VIII. If the final decision of any general body thus constituted shall seem to any Synod within it in conflict with the faith, involving violation of the rights of conscience, it is the duty of that Synod to take such steps as shall be needed to prevent a compromise on its part with error. To this end it may withdraw itself from relations which make it responsible for departure from the faith of the Gospel, or for an equivocal attitude towards it. Such steps should not be taken on any but well defined grounds of conscience, not on mere suspicion, nor until prayerful, earnest and repeated efforts to correct the wrong have proved useless, and no remedy remains but withdrawal."*

1) The decisions of such a body must be really final and beyond all reasonable hope of correction before the withdrawal occurs.

2) These fixed and final decisions must involve matters of faith and conscience: even final decisions in regard to questions out of the sphere of conscience, questions about adiaphora and polity, do not justify the withdrawal of Synods which are dissatisfied with those decisions.

3) The steps needed to correct the evil supposed will vary according to the circumstance.

4) Ecclesiastical government rests upon the conscience of men, and hence demands a purity and freedom of conscience which the State cannot in its ideal embrace.

5) At this point it may be of help to us to state clearly and definitely the true character of *Lutheran Church Government*, as implied by the principles so far advanced.

1. The Lutheran Church, through her heavenly Head, as King and Lord of all, and through His rule, in consequence, is *a pure monarchy*—yet she is not in her human government a monarchy under an earthly head as the Romish Church is, but a communion of the universal priesthood, representing itself in the office of the ministry (in which Christ also represents Himself toward His Church) and in other ways, but acknowledging no earthly head or ruler.

2. She is *not a hierarchy*, though she is under a sacred rule and acknowledges the ministry, as the representative of the order which forms with the domestic and civil orders, the three great divine institutions. She has no hierarchy in the *autocratic* sense, like that of the *Jus divinum* hierarchy of the Episcopal Churches. For even where she has bishops (and that too with the so-called Apostolical Succession, as in Sweden and Norway) their powers are limited and representative, and they claim no *divine* right not common to all ministers of the Word.

3. She is not an *aristocracy* like the Presbyterian Church, in which virtually a body of chosen men rule the congregation for life; nor like the Methodist Episcopal Church which is ruled by its clergy who are not chosen by the people; for in the Lutheran Church the people choose their own pastors, and represent themselves not only generically by their pastors, but directly and specifically in all her deliberative bodies by delegates.

4. She is not a *sporadic Polyarchy*, like the Independents, separate congregations ruled by the multitude, but maintains a proper unity of the Church, and a subordinate but real authority of the ministers of the Word and of bodies of ministers and by delegates representing many congregations.

5. The Lutheran Church Government may be called *Christo-cratic Representative Government.*

a) It is *Christocratic* on its divine side. All legislative or lawgiving power in the sphere of conscience is vested in Christ. Her law is already made by Christ her Head, is recorded in Holy Scripture, and is supreme and unchangeable.

b) It is, however, on its human side, representative and elective. She has power for making regulations for the better understanding and more perfect carrying out of fundamental, unchangeable constitutional law.

c) There is also a subordinate law-interpreting, law-applying and law-executing authority in the Church. This she exercises representatively through the ministry and through bodies composed of ministers and others, and this representation is elective.

d) This authority, though not absolute like the law-giving power, but limited and ministerial, nevertheless, is real, and to all who voluntarily remain under it, decisive.

"IX. The obligation, under which congregations consent to place themselves, to conform to the decisions of Synods, does not rest on any assumption that Synods are infallible, but on the supposition that the decisions have been so guarded by wise constitutional provisions as to create a higher moral probability of their being true and rightful than the decisions in conflict with them, which may be made by single congregations or individuals. All final decisions should be guarded with the utmost care, so that they shall in no case claim without just grounds to be the judgment of those congregations in whose name and by whose authority they are made—in the absence of which just grounds they are null and void."

1) No government, civil or ecclesiastical, synodical or congregational, can truly rest upon an assumption of infallibility.

2) The admission of fallibility does not destroy rightful authority either in the State, in the Church or in the Family.

3) Some have objected that to accept the decisions of Synods involves a transfer on the part of the people of their own rights divinely given them, and hence are not capable of transfer. The answer is simply this: one of the inalienable rights of the people is the right to represent themselves, and they do not transfer their rights to representatives, but only exercise them more perfectly through them.

4) Others have objected that such authority as we grant to Synods is inconsistent with the supremacy of the Bible as the Rule of faith. We grant that no governing body has an independent authority over the conscience, and all decisions bind the conscience only because they are conformed to the Word of God—so far and no farther.

5) The authority claimed for Synods is not in conflict with the right of private judgment.

6) It is not in conflict with the right of minorities.

a) The minority has the right of debate; *b*) the right of protest; *c*) the right of withdrawal, after the final failure of all modes of redress, when the wrong involves matters of faith or of moral principles.

7. Though it is possible that a minority may be right, this does not settle the question.

a) There must be government of some kind. If a final decision is to be made, it is unanimous, or the minority must rule the majority, or the majority rule the minority.

b) All other things being equal, it is more probable that a minority is wrong than that the majority is wrong.

c) If the many may not rule because a minority may be right, then all government of the Family, of the State or of the Church goes to the ground, and we are left in anarchy.

d) Such postulates, starting in an extreme and mistaken Protestantism, or ultra Congregationalism, or Individualism, prepare the minds of men for Romanism, for she postulates and assumes that we are not to establish authority unless we can prove it to be infallible.

e) Men get weary of arguing that as no government is infallible they will do without any, and in the feeling of the misery of such a position, are ready to rush to Rome because she claims infallibility.

8) Constitutions should carefully define the circumstances under which decisions are final beyond all possibility of repeal.

9) To refer questions, decided by general bodies, to the individual congregations, is to overthrow the whole proper intent of such general bodies. They may freely refer questions to distinct Synods, or congregations, or individuals, for their well considered advice; and there may be classes of questions which for good reasons may be required, by the Constitution, to be specially referred, but as the normal and ordinary rule it is wrong,—the very existence of general bodies involving the assumption that the conjoint deliberation of the congregations represented is more likely to reach results which the deliberate final judgment of the congregations will approve than if they acted separately.

10) Congregations may demand constitutional provisions for the reservation of certain classes of topics entirely for themselves, for the references of other questions to them, and for the opinions of the congregations previous to decisions.

11) No congregation has the right to instruct a delegate to speak or vote contrary to his conscience, nor to instruct him to

vote in a certain way in any case, while it is possible that an intelligent conviction might impel him to vote in another way. Those who represent the congregation are to listen in its place, calmly weigh facts for it, allow the proper influence of argument, and in no case to vote in conflict with their conscientious convictions.

"X. In the formation of a general body, the Synods may know and deal with each other only as Synods. In such case the official record is to be accepted as evidence of the doctrinal position of each Synod, and of the principles for which alone the other Synods become responsible by connection with it."

"XI. The leading objects for which Synods should be organized are:

"1. The maintenance and diffusion of sound doctrine, as the same is taught in God's Word and confessed in the authorized standards of the Church.

"2. When controversies arise in regard to articles of faith, to decide them in accordance with God's Word and the pure confessions of that Word.

"3. The proper regulation of the human externals of worship, that the same, in character and administration, may be in keeping with the spirit of the New Testament and with the liberty of the Church, and may edify the Body of Christ.

"4. The maintenance of pure discipline, to the fostering of holiness and fidelity in the ministry and people.

"5. The devising and executing of wise and Scriptural counsels and plans for carrying on the work of the Church, in every department of beneficent labor for the souls and bodies of men at home and abroad.

"All these things are to be done, that the saving power of the Gospel may be realized, that good order may be maintained, and that all unsoundness in faith and life may be averted, that God may be glorified, and that Christ our King may rule in a pure, peaceful and active Church."

Two extreme views of the ideal Lutheran Church Polity.

1. Among the many able works on Lutheran Church Polity which have appeared within the last fifty years, two of them that take the highest rank represent directly opposite views.

2. Stahl, one of the most illustrious jurists and statesmen of his day, in his masterly work *Die Kirchenverfassung, etc.* (2d ed., 1862,) presents the hierarchical view, while Walther in his able work *Kirche und Amt* (2d ed., 1865,) emphasizes the rights of the congregation.

3. In order that we may clearly understand the points of the controversy at issue, we will present Stahl's criticism of the views of Dr. Walther and of the Missouri Synod, largely as a matter of historical interest.

Stahl's review of Walther's Kirche und Amt.

1. "Prof. Walther, who holds the chair of Theology at St. Louis, attempts a sort of genuine middle way between the theory that the ministry is from God and the ministry is from the congregation."

2. "He lays down these theses:

" 'I. The Holy Ministry or Pastorate is an office distinct from the priestly office which all believers have.'

" 'II. The Ministry or Pastorate is no human arrangement, but an office founded by God Himself.'

" 'III. The ministry is no arbitrary office, but an office whose establishment is enjoined upon the Church and to which the Church, under ordinary circumstances, is bound to the end of time.' "

3. "Again he lays down the following theses:

" 'VI. The ministry is committed by God through the congregation, which is the possessor of all Church power, or the power of the keys, and through its divinely prescribed call.' ...

" 'VII. The Holy Ministry is the power committed by God through the congregation as the possessor of the priesthood and of all Church power, to exercise the rights of the spiritual priesthood in a public office in the common interest.' "

4. Stahl comments as follows:

1) "Consequently Walther teaches the divine institution of the office, and yet at the same time the derivation of its rights and powers by consignment of the congregation as their original possessor."

2) "In this doctrine the idea of a congregational assignment is totally unnecessary. Hoeflinghad need of it, because he does not recognize the office as of God and considers the office as given in the universal priesthood. But if the office be one distinct from the priesthood, and is, as such, instituted of God Himself, what need is there of a derivation of its authority from a congregational assignment?.... In this doctrine the idea of a congregational assignment is without significance and vain. What does it amount to, what interest is subserved, by saying that the congregation has committed to it the powers of the office, when it is yet God's arrangement that these powers should be exercised through the office, and that the congregation itself dare not exercise them?.... Only in one case can it involve any interests and cease to be useless, to wit, when it is claimed, that the congregation from which the power is derived, stands above the office, and though it dare not itself exercise the powers, yet can sit in judgment on the way in which they are exercised through the office, and make a new arrangement."

3. "This idea of popular sovereignty was laid down already in the parochial order of Missouri (1839, 1840), according to which 'the congregation is the supremest and last tribunal in the Church and has the right to depose its preachers.' "

4. "In this practical result, this doctrine amounts to about the same as Hoefling's."

5. "The argument for the doctrine is no better than its substance. Walther produces two proofs for it:

    1) That the keys were given by God immediately to the congregation;

    2) That the Apostle Matthias and the deacons were elected by the whole multitude of the assembled believers.

6. Walther says: "As the congregation or assembly of believers has the keys and the priesthood immediately (Matt. 18:15–20; 1 Pet. 2:5–10), it is it and can be none but it, through which, to wit, by its election, call, and sending, the ministry, which openly administers the office of the keys and all priestly functions in the congregation, is committed to certain properlyfitted persons. Hence also we read that the Apostle Matthias himself was chosen not by the eleven alone, but by the whole multitude of believers (Acts 1:15–26)."

7. Stahl says: "The first statement that the keys were given immediately to the congregation is no proof, but merely an assertion of the thing to be proved. It is a begging of the question. From the passages quoted from Scripture it follows as we have shown (in his own work), not that the keys were immediately given to the Church and then only transferred from the Church to the office, but in accord with the commonly received exposition, *that they were given to the organized Church and consequently immediately by God to the office, the ministry as the executive member in it.*"

(Here Stahl presents his own theory).

8. Stahl continues: "Now by the congregation Walther certainly understands actual believers, 'those who stand with Peter upon the rock,'—consequently the invisible Church, and not the Church as an institution. There is thus lacking every application to the congregation actually established and the validity of the ministry throughout hinges upon the question whether the congregation assigning it actually stands upon the rock."

9. As to the second argument Stahl remarks: "The second proof, that according to the N.T. narrative the congregation had the appointment of officers, is not historically correct, not even with the mitigation which Walther adds, that the ministry already existing in these congregations had a part in these elections. It is placed beyond all doubt that in the Apostolic and subsequent era the congregation did not have the appointment, but only a concurrence in the appointment, and that the authority of the existing office, not merely that existing in this or that particular congregation, but of the office existing in the Church in general, formed an essential factor for this, not merely as consenting, but as testing and confirming, and in the proper sense, assigning the office."

10. Stahl continues: "If it were historically correct as Walther puts it, nay if we had an express and clear command of God, that the congregations were to choose the preachers by mere numerical majorities and independent of every testing and confirmation by a higher authority, still the derivation of the powers from an assignment on the part of the congregation would not follow from this. Two wholly distinct things are here confounded, one that the congregations choose the persons for

the office, and the other that the authority of the office is derived from the congregation."

11. Further on he says: "Walther has the merit of having collected from the sources rich material on the subject of his book. He has also, as it seems, put forth an honest effort to moderate the radical tendency. But these unimportant mitigations, which do not affect the principles in question, offer no barrier to radicalism, but on the contrary, aid it."

12. After characterizing in general the tendency of Missouri, he adds: "The congregation is the highest, the ultimate tribunal in the Church, and the preachers are its servants, and accountable to it. Then further is brought forward the Calvinistic fable that according to God's Word, lay-elders were given the congregations of the Apostolic Church, who then administered their office by divine right, in virtue of the divine institution of it, and as representative of the congregation ordained by it."

13. After a still further description of this congregational rule, Stahl adds: "This is nothing more than the North-American Democracy and the spirit of the Declaration of Independence transferred to the Church, and this is given out as Lutheranism."

Some Annotations on Stahl's Review of Walther.

1. If the Democracy of America has had its influence on Walther, the absoluteness of the Court has also tinged Stahl.

2. Both the theory of Walther and the criticism of Stahl must stand upon their own merits, without reference to the political theories with which each may be in consonance.

3. Dr. Walther and the Missouri Synod certainly deserve the most cordial admiration for their effort to bring forth the congregational life of our Lutheran Church in this country. In this they must command the heartiest sympathy even of those who cannot accept all their theories, nor justify all their measures.

4. Stahl's acquaintance with the governmental views and practice of our country does not seem to be very deep. Nothing is remoter from the spirit of our Constitution, both as a nation and State, than the idea of a direct, unmixed democracy.

5. The ideal government in the Missouri Synod is not the ideal of our American Fathers of early times, nor of our great statesmen, nor of the sober part of our people. The government of America is not a simple democracy, but is republican. The people

in no instance rule directly. No assembly of the people makes the laws, enforces the laws, or executes the laws. We have a representative law-giving body, a representative law-enforcing body, and a representative executive. And in every case our representatives are not merely mechanical organs of the popular will, but they are representative of the people.

6. The excess of the principle of popular sovereignty, congregational independency, is doubtless the result of reaction against pressure, and is in consonance with a certain extravagance and one sidedness which are the defects of the entire Missouri tendency.

7. On the question of the lay-eldership, Dr. Walther and his Synod have fallen into a lamentable mistake, which will go far to cast suspicion upon the thoroughness of their learning and the soundness of their reasoning in every direction on the question of the ministry.

BIBLIOGRAPHY

The Literature of the Doctrine of the Church is very extensive. McElhinney, in his work on *The Doctrine of the Church*, gives a list of 873 titles up to 1870, while Dexter, in his standard work, *Congregationalism as seen in its Literature*, gives the titles and bibliographical notes of 7, 250 books, covering the period from 1546 to 1879. We will refer to very few of these, unless standard works, limiting the list to the more important books on this subject published since, and arranging them under special topics.

1. *General Works*

1. *Ante-Nicene Fathers.* 10 vols. 1885–1896.
2. Bennett, *Christian Archæology.* 2d ed. 1898.
3. Landon, *Manual of Councils of the Holy Catholic Church.* 2 vols. 2d ed. 1893.
4. Neander (Robinson), *Planting and Training of the Christian Church.* 1864.
5. *Nicene and Post-Nicene Fathers.* First Series. 14 vols. 1886–1890.
6. *Nicene and Post-Nicene Fathers.* Second Series. 14 vols. 1890–1900.
7. Richter, *Lehrbuch des kath. und evang. Kirchenrechts,* 9th ed., by Kahl, 1886.
8. Schaff, *Creeds of Christendom.* 3 vols. 1881.
9. Schaff-Herzog, *Encyclopœdia.* 3 vols. 1882.
10. Smith and Cheetham, *Dictionary of Christian Antiquities.* 2 vols. 1876.
11. Smith and Wace, *Dictionary of Christian Biography.* 4 vols. 1877.

2. *History of Doctrines*

1. Cunningham, *Historical Theology*, etc. 2 vols. 2d ed. 1864.
2. Crippen, *Popular Introd. to History of Christian Doctrine.* 1883.
3. Fisher, *History of Christian Doctrine.* 1896.
4. Hagenbach, *History of Doctrines* (H. B. Smith). 2 vols. 1861.
5. Hagenbach, *History of Doctrines* (Plumptre). 3 vols. 1880, 1881.
6. Neander, *History of Christian Dogmas.* 2 vols. 1878.
7. Schmid, *Lehrbuch des Dogmengeschichte.* 4th ed. 1887.
8. Seeberg, *Lehrbuch des Dogmengeschichte.* 2 vols. 1895, 1898.
9. Sheldon, *History of Christian Doctrine.* 2 vols. 1885.
10. Thomasius, *Die Dogmengeschichte*, etc. 2 vols. 1874, 1876.

3. *General Doctrinal Works*

1) *Baptist*

1. Boyce, *Abstract of Systematic Theology.* 1887.
2. Dagg, *Manual of Theology.* 1859.
3. Hovey, *Manual of Systematic Theology*, etc. 1877.
4. Johnson, *Outline of Systematic Theology.* 1891.
5. Strong, *Systematic Theology.* 4th ed. 1893.

2) *Congregational*

6. Denney, *Studies in Theology.* 1895.
7. Fairbairn, *Place of Christ in Modern Theology.* 1890.
8. Finney, *Lectures on Systematic Theology.* 1878.
9. Pond, Lectures on Christian Theology. 1867.
10. Stearns, *Present Day Theology.* 1893.

3) *Disciples of Christ* (Christians, or Campbellites, or Campbellite Baptists)

11. Campbell, Alex., *The Christian System.*

4) *(Dutch) Reformed Church in America*

12. Kuyper, *The Work of the Holy Spirit.* 1900.
13. Van Oosterzee, *Christian Dogmatics.* 2 vols. 1874.

5) *Church of England (Episcopal)*

14. Buel, *Systematic Theology*. 1889.
15. Cutts, *Some Chief Truths of Religion*.
16. Hooker, *Ecclesiastical Polity* (1594). 3 vols. 1845.
17. Maclear, *Introduction to the Creeds*. 1895.
18. Maclear and Williams, *Introduction to the Articles of Church, of England*. 1895.
19. Mason, *The Faith of the Gospel*. 1887.
20. Moule, *Outlines of Christian Doctrine*. 1892.
21. Norris, *Rudiments of Theology*. 1876.
22. Pearson, *Exposition of the Creed* (1659), 1859.
23. Percival, *A Digest of Theology*. 1893.
24. Sadler, *Church Doctrine, Bible Truth*. 1869.
25. Strong, Thomas B., *Manual of Theology*. 1893.

6) *(German) Reformed Church*

26. Ebrard, *Christ. Dogmatic*. 2d. ed. 2 vols. 1863.
27. Gerhart, *Institutes of the Christian Religion*. 2 vols. 1891–94.
28. Heppe, *Dogm. der evang. reform. Kirche*. 1861.
29. Lange, *Christ. Dogmatik*. 3 vols. 1870.

7) *Mediating Lutheran*

30. Dorner, *System of Christian Doctrine*. 4 vols. 1880–82.
31. Martensen, *Christian Dogmatics*. 1866.
32. Nitzsch, *System of Christian Doctrine*. 1849.
33. Rothe, *Theologische Ethik*. 2d ed. 5 vols. 1867–62.

8) *Confessional Lutheran*

34. Baier, *Compendium Theol. Positivœ*. (Walther). 3 vols. 1879.
35. Bjorling, *Den Christ. Dogmatiken*. (Swedish). 3 vols. 1866.
36. Bring, *Christ. Troslaeran*. Lund, 1877.
37. Frank, *System der Christ. Wahrheit*. 3d. ed. 2 vols. 1894.
38. Hase, *Hutterus Redivivus*, 12th ed. 1883.
39. Jacobs, *Elements of Religion*. 1894.
40. Johnson, *Grundrids of den Syst. Theologi*. (Norwegian).
41. Krauth, *Conservative Reformation*. 1871.
42. Lindberg, *Encheiridion i Dogmatik*. 1898. (Swedish).
43. Luthardt, *Die Christ. Glaubenslehre*. 1898.

44. Luthardt, *Kompendiumder Dogmatik.* 10th ed. 1900.
45. Oettingen, *Luth. Dogmatik.* 2 vols. 1897–99.
46. Philippi, *Kirch. Glaubenslehre.* 6 vols. 3d ed. 1883–90.
47. Schmid, *Doct. Theology of the Lutheran Church.* 3d ed. 1899.
48. Thomasius, *Christi Person und Werk.* 3d ed. 2 vols. 1888.
49. Vilmar, *Dogmatik.* 2 vols. 1874.

   9) *Methodist*

50. Field, *Handbook of Christian Theology.* 1887
51. Foster, *Studies in Theology.* 3 vols. 1881.
52. Miley, *Systematic Theology.* 2 vols. 1894.
53. Pope, *Compendium of Christian Theology.* 3 vols. 1881.
54. Pope, *Higher Catechism of Theology.* 1884.
55. Raymond, *Systematic Theology.* 3 vols. 1879.
56. Watson, *Theological Institutes.* 2 vols. 1850.

   10) *Moravians.*

57. Plitt, *Evangelische Glaubenslehre.* 2 vols. 1863.

   11) *Presbyterian*

58. Calvin, *Institutes of the Christian Religion.* 3 vols. 1846.
59. Dabney, *Theology, Dogmatic and Polemic,* 3d ed. 1885.
60. Hodge, A. A., *Outlines of Theology.* 1882.
61. Hodge, Charles, *Systematic Theology.* 3 vols. 1873.
62. Shedd, *Dogmatic Theology.* 3 vols. 1894.
63. Smith, H. B., *System of Christian Theology.* 1892.

   12) *Roman Catholic*

64. Aquinas, Thomas, *Summa Theologicæ.* 8 vols. 1876.
65. Berington and Kirk, *Faith of Catholics Confirmed, etc.* 3 vols. 1885.
66. Di Bruno, *Catholic Belief.* 1900.
67. Gibbons, *Faith of our Fathers.* 36th ed. 1890
68. Hunter, *Outlines of Dogmatic Theology.* 3 vols. 1898.
69. Hurter, *Theologicæ Dogmaticæ Compendium.* 3 vols. 5th ed. 1885.
70. Perrone, *Praelectiones Theologiæ Compendium, Redactæ.* 2 vols. 36th ed. 1881.

71. Schouppe, *Course of Religious Instruction for Catholic Colleges, etc.*
72. Searle, *Plain Facts, etc.* 426th thousand. 1902.
73. Tanquerey, *Theologia Fundamentalis* (Aquinas). 1 vol.
74. Tanquerey, *Theologia Specialis* (Aquinas). 2 vols.
75. Wiseman, *Priyiciple, Doctrines and Practices of the Catholic Church.* 6th ed. 1862.

13) *Greek Catholic*

76. Macaire, *Theologie Dogmatique Orthodoxe.* 2 vols. 1859. Paris.

4. *Special Works on the Church and Church Polity.*

1) *Episcopal or Anglican*

1. Bilson, *Perpetual Government of Christ's Church.* (1593), 1842.
2. Field, *Of the Church. Five Books.* (1606–1610.) 4 vols, 1854.
3. Gore, *The Church and the Ministry.* 1893.
4. Haddan, *Apostolic Succession in the Church of England.* 1869.
5. Hatch, *Organization of the Early Christian Churches.* 1880.
6. Jacob, *The Ecclesiastical Polity of the N.T.* 1872.
7. Jewel, *Apology of the Church of England.* (1562.) Often. (25 cents.)
8. Lightfoot, "The Christian Ministry" in *Comm. on Philippians.* 1868.
9. Maurice, *Kingdom of Christ.* 2 vols. 1842.
10. McElhinney, *The Doctrine of the Church. A Historical Monograph.* 1871.
11. Nowell, *Catechism.* (1570), 1839.
12. Palmer, *A Treatise on the Church of Christ.* 2 vols. 1842.
13. Salmon, *The Infallibility of the Church.* 1888.

2) *Congregationalism*

14. Cathcart, *Baptist Encyclopœdia.* 1880.
15. Cummings, *Dictionary of Congregational Usages and Principles.* 5th ed. 1854.
16. Dale, *Manual of Congregatioyial Principles.* 1884.

17. Dagg, *Church Order* (Baptist). 1859.
18. Dexter, *Congregationalism, etc.* 5th ed. 1879.
19. Dexter, *Congregationalism ... as seen in its Literature.* 1880.
20. Ladd, *Principles of Church Polity.* 1882.
21. Reynolds (Editor), *Ecclesia, Church Problems, etc.* (Congregational.) 2 vols. 1870, 1871.
22. Rogers, *Church Systems in England in 19th Cent.* 1881.
23. Walker, *Creeds and Platforms of Congregationalism.* 1893.
24. Wayland, *Principles and Practices of the Baptists.* 1857.

3) *Lutheran Protestantism*

25. Beste, *Martin Luther's Glaubetislehre.* Halle. 1845.
26. Delitzsch, *Vier Buecher von der Kirche.* 1847.
27. Dieckhoff, *Luther's Lehre v. der Kirchl. Gewalt.* 1865.
28. *Distinctive Doctrines and Usages of the Evang. Luth, Church, in U. S.* 1893.
29. Dove-Richter, *Lehrb. d. Kathol. u. evang. Kirchen-rechts.,* 7th ed. 1874.
30. Graul, *Distinctive Doctries, etc.* 1897.
31. Harless, *Kirche and Amt nach luth. Lehre.* 1853.
32. Harless, *Etliche gewissenfragen, Kirche, Kirchenamt, etc.* 1862.
33. Harnack, *Die Kirche, ihr Amt., etc.* 1862.
34. Harnack, *Praktische Theologie.* 2 vols. 1877.
35. Von Hofmann, *Vermischte Aufsaetze.* 1878.
36. Hoefling. *Grund. der evang. luth. Kirchenverfassung.* ed. 3. 1853.
37. Jacobs, *Book of Concord.* 2 vols. 1882, 1883.
38. Jacobs and Haas, *Lutheran Cyclopedia.* 1899.
39. Kliefoth, *Acht Buecher von der Kirche.* 1854.
40. Koestlin, *Luther's Lehre von der Kirche.* 1853.
41. Koestlin, *Theology of Luther.* 2 vols. 1897.
42. Loehe, *Drei Bucher von der Kirche, etc.* 1845.
43. Loehe, *Aphorismen ueber die N.T. Aemter, etc.* 1849.
44. Loehe, *Kirche und Amt, neue Aphorismen.* 1853.
45. Loy, *The Christian Church, etc.* 1896.
46. Mueller, *Die Symbolische Buecher.* 7th ed. 1890.
47. Muenchmeyer, *Das Amt. des N.T., etc.* 1853.

48. Muenchmeyer, *Das Dogma der sicht. und unsicht. Kirche.* 1854.

49. Richter, *Geschichle der Evang. Kirchenverfassung.* 1851.

50. Stahl, *Die Kirchenfassung nach Lehre und Recht der Prot.* 2d ed. 1862.

51. Stahl, *Die Luth. Kirche und die Union.* 2d ed. 1860.

52. Walther, *Die Stimme unserer Kirche.... Kirche und Amt.* 2d ed. 1865.

53. Zezschwitz, *System der Prakt. Theologie.* 1878.

4) *Presbyterianism*

54. Anderson, *Defence of the Church Government ... of the Presbyterians.* (1714), 1820.

55. Bannerman, (James,) *The Church of Christ, etc.* 2 vols. 1868.

56. Bannerman, (Douglas), *The Scripture Doctrine of the Church.* 1887.

57. Binnie, *The Church.* 1882.

58. Brown, *Vindication of the Presb. Form of Ch. Government.* 1805.

59. Candlish, *The Kingdom of God, etc.* 1884.

60. Coleman, *Ancient Christianity Exemplified.* 1875.

61. Coleman, *Manual on Prelacy and Ritualism, etc.* 1871.

62. Corwin, *A Manual of the Reformed Church in America.* 4th ed. 1902.

63. Cunningham, *Discussion on Church Principles, etc.* 1863.

64. Hodge, *Constitutional History of the Presbyterian Church.* 2 vols. 1839–40.

65. Hodge, *Discussions on Church Polity.* 1879.

66. Killen, *The Framework of the Church, etc.* 1890.

67. King, *Defence of the Presb. Form of Ch. Government.* 1854.

68. McGill, *Church Government.* 1889.

69. Miller and Lorimer, *Manual of Presbytery.* 1842.

70. Morris, *Ecclesiology, a Treatise on the Church, etc.* 1885.

71. Withrow, *Form of the Christian Temple.* 1889.

5) *Roman Catholicism*

72. Addis and Arnold, *Catholic Dictionary.* 3d ed. 1884.

73. Barnum, *Romanism as it is.* 1877.

74. *Catechism of Council of Trent* (Trans, by Buckley). 1852.

75. Chemnitz, *Examen Concilii Tridentini* (German trans.). 1875
76. Cramp, *A Text-Book of Popery.* 1831.
77. Doellinger, *Declarations and Letters on Vatican Degrees.* 1891.
78. Gore, *Roman Catholic Claims.* 1889.
79. James, *Corruptions of Scripture, Councils and Fathers* (Cox). 1843.
80. Littledale, *Plain Reasons Against Joining Rome.* 1881.
81. Littledale, *The Petrine Claims.* 1889.
82. Moehler, *Symbolism.* 1844.
83. *Roman Symbols.* In Schaff's *Creeds of Christendom.* Vol. 2.
84. Specht, *Die Lehre von der Kirche, etc.* 1892.

EXAMINATION QUESTIONS
ON
ECCLESIOLOGY

1. The Doctrine concerning the Church.

1. Why is this subject so important?

2. How may we define the Church according to her spiritual essence?

3. What is the Church as an external organization?

4. Distinguish between the Roman and the Protestant conception of the Church.

I. THE SCRIPTURE DOCTRINE

5. What three Hebrew words are used in the O.T. to designate the congregation of the people?

6. What Greek words are used in the Septuagint?

7. How may we distinguish between *qahal* and *edha?*

8. How is the word *Synagogue* used in the N.T.?

9. In what three senses is the word *ecclesia* used in the N.T.?

10. What is the derivation of the word *church?*

11. Show that the word *ecclesia* in the N.T. is often used to denote the entire Church universal.

12. Show that it is also often used to designate local congregations.

a) The Teaching of Jesus

13. How does Christ use the word *church* in Matt. 16:18?

14. In Matt. 18:17?

15. What is the great lesson of the Parable of the Sower?

16. Of the Parable of the Tares?

17. Of the Parable of the Mustard Seed?

19. Of the Hidden Treasure?

20. Of the Pearl of great Price?

21. Of the Draw-net?

22. Distinguish between the Church and the Kingdom of God.

23. Show that Christ regards His Kingdom as present and yet also as future.

24. Show that the Church has a divine origin.

25. In what sense is it Christ's Kingdom?

26. Quote and explain Luke 17:20.

27. Illustrate the close union between Christ and the Church.

28. In what sense is the Church a Kingdom on earth?

29. Show that the Church embraces heaven and earth.

30. Distinguish between *this æon* and that *which is to come.*

31. Show that there is even now a kingdom of God *in heaven.*

32. Trace the order of Christ's establishing of His Church.

33. Prove that Christ maintains and guides His Church.

34. What signs give manifestation of the existence of the Church?

35. Show that the Word of God is essentially the basis of the Church.

36. Show that baptism is also the way to Christ.

37. How are the Word and Baptism connected in bringing men into the Kingdom?

38. How are the Word and the Lord's Supper connected in strengthening believers?

39. Name the three means of grace.

40. Show that in the Church on earth there is a mixture of good and evil.

41. Show that there is a difference between the ministry and the laity.

42. Show that the destruction of Jerusalem became an epoch in the development of the Church.

43. What is the great lesson of the Parable of "the Seed growing secretly?"

44. On what does the development of the Church largely depend?

45. Of how many epochs in the development of the Church may we speak?

46. What is meant by the last epoch?

47. In what sense is the Parousia a continuous judgment?

48. How does it differ from the final judgment?

49. When was the Church of Christ properly founded?

b) *The Teaching of the Apostles*

50. How, according to Peter, can we become members of the Church of Christ?

51. How is the unity and growth of the Church promoted?

52. What figure does Peter use to illustrate the building up of the Church?

53. Explain fully 1 Pet. 2:9, 10.

54. Show that the Church includes believing Jews and converted Gentiles.

55. In what sense is Christ both Shepherd and Bishop of souls?

56. Where does Paul develop the doctrine of the Church?

57. In what three senses does Paul use the word *ecclesia.*

58. Show that Paul lays great stress upon baptism as the means of putting us into living fellowship with Christ.

59. Show that believers became one body in Christ.

60. Show that the first churches were house congregations.

61. What did the Church in a city comprise?

62. What is meant by the *actual* Church?

63. What is meant by the *ideal* Church?

64. Explain Paul's figure, that the Church is a *spiritual house* (1 Cor. 3:9–15).

65. Explain Eph. 2:20–22.

66. What figure with reference to the Church does Paul prefer?

67. Develop his teaching on this point.

68. Distinguish between Paul's teaching that the Church is the body of Christ, and that Christ is the head of the Church.

69. Develop Paul's teaching that the Church is the bride of Christ.

70. When will the marriage take place?

71. In what sense is the Church the pillar and ground of the truth (1 Tim. 3:15)?

72. On what does the existence and perpetuation of the Church depend?

73. Summarize the teaching of John.

II. THE CHURCH DOCTRINE

1. *The Ancient Catholic Church*

74. What two aspects of the Church have been recognized from the beginning?

75. Upon what aspect did the early Church lay stress?

76. What three great names are identified with the Ante-Nicene development of the doctrine of the Church?

77. What position did Ignatius take?

78. When did he die?

79. Of what kind of episcopacy does Ignatius speak?

80. When did Irenæus die?

81. How does he regard the Episcopacy?

82. Why was he so anxious to make out a list of bishops in Rome?

83. How does Hatch sum up the tendency at the close of the second century?

84. What do the Early Fathers teach concerning the Church?

85. What position did Cyprian take?

86. What is the date of his death?

87. What is his theory of the unity of the Church?

88. Explain more fully his theory of the sacerdotal hierarchy of the bishops.

89. What does he regard as the source of the unity of the Church?

90. How does the bishop receive his authority?

91. What distinction may be drawn between the words *ecclesia* and *congregation?*

92. How many congregations were established in a city in early Christian times?

93. What names were given to the pastors of congregations?

94. How are the words Bishop and Presbyter used in the N.T.?

95. What is meant by *Jus divinum* Presbyterianism?

96. By *Jus divinum diocesan* Episcopacy?

97. How many ministerial offices are known in the N.T.?

98. When did the first distinction rise between the terms *elder* and *bishop?*

99. Trace the origin of the *congregational* Episcopate.

100. Trace the development of the *diocesan* Episcopate.

101. What can we say of the succession of Bishops at Rome?

102. What was Cyprian's fundamental error?

103. Show that the Church was, after all, regarded as essentially *invisible.*

104. How does the Apostles' Creed express this?

105. The Nicene Creed?

I. *The Unity of the Church*

106. What does Scripture teach concerning the *unity* of the Church?

107. In what five figures is this unity set forth?

108. In what way was this true idea of unity soon perverted?

109. In what treatise did Cyprian develop his peculiar doctrine?

110. Explain and trace the change in meaning in the three following formulas:
Scripture: Out of *Christ* there is no salvation.
Cyprian: Out of the *Church* there is no salvation.
Rome: Out of the *Roman Church* there is no salvation.

111. What did Augustine teach?

112. What event contradicted this conception of the external unity of the Church?

II. *The Holiness of the Church*

113. In what sense do we not ascribe holiness to the Church?

114. Why do we ascribe holiness to the Church?

115. What does Augustine teach concerning the Church?

III. *The Catholicity of the Church*

116. What is the meaning of the word *Catholic?*

117. Why is the word *Christian* the best translation covering its true meaning?

118. Where do we first find the phrase *Catholic Church?*

119. How do the Early Fathers use the word *Catholic* in respect to place?

120. In respct to time?

121. In respect to teaching?

122. Show that in virtue of its true universality the Christian Church has a unity which excludes any and all particular churches which have risen in time or may fall in time.

123. Show that all particular pure churches together do not make up the Church Universal.

IV. *The Apostolicity of the Church*

124. Prove from Eph. 2:20 that the Church is Apostolic.

125. In what sense may we regard the Church Apostolic?

126. Why did the Early Fathers emphasize the Apostolicity of the Church?

127. How does Tertullian develop this?

128. Where does Augustine treat of this subject?

129. To what did this train of thinking finally lead?

130. Why is this conception of the Apostolicity of the Church erroneous?

131. In what sense and how far may the Church be regarded as Apostolic?

V. *Montanism. Etc*

132. Define Montanism.

133. What was its special aim?

134. What its errors?

135. What was the tendency known as Novatianism?

136. What was Donatism?

137. What distinctions was Augustine compelled to make in his conflict with the Donatists?

II. THE ROMAN CATHOLIC CHURCH.

138. What does the Roman Catholic Church teach concerning the Church?

139. What does Hildebrand teach?

140. What does Boniface VIII. teach?

141. What was the position taken by Thomas Aquinas?

142. By Perrone?

143. What does the Roman Catechism teach?

144. Who is the greatest of all Roman controversialists?

145. What does this writer teach of the Church?

146. What does Pope Leo XIII. teach?

147. Name the four characteristics of the Roman Catholic Church, according to the Roman theory.

148. Name her four marks, according to the Roman theory.

149. How does the Roman Church define the unity of the Church?

150. How is the Holiness of the Church defined?

151. How is the Catholicity of the Church defined?

152. How is the Apostolicity of the Church defined?

153. How many marks does Bellarmine ascribe to the Roman Catholic Church?

154. On what two grounds do Roman Catholic theologians defend the Supremacy of the Pope?

155. State their argument on the ground of *reason*, and answer it.

156. State the four reasons, on the ground of *authority*, on which the Catholic theologians rely, to prove the Supremacy of the Pope.

157. In general, what three statements may be made in reply?

158. On what three passages of Scripture does the Roman Church base this doctrine?

159. Why cannot John 21:15–17 be used to establish their theory of Peter's Jurisdiction?

160. Why cannot Luke 22:31, 32 be used to establish their doctrine of Peter's infallibility and primacy?

161. What does Plumptre say of the Roman exegesis of Matt. 16:18?

162. How many general reasons are given to show that the Roman theory cannot be deduced from Matt. 16:18?

163. State the first three reasons?

164. Show that the whole recorded history of the Early Church is opposed to such a theory.

165. Illustrate by two historical events recorded in the early chapters of Acts.

166. Name three other important historical events recorded in Acts that show that Peter did not have such a supremacy.

167. Show that Peter himself never claimed such authority.

168. Show that Paul does not recognize nor know of any such supremacy.

169. Show that certain events in Peter's personal life prove the falsity of the Roman theory.

170. Why is there no foundation whatever for such a theory?

171. Show that the Roman interpretation of the word *rock* in Matt. 16:18 cannot be established (Five points).

172. What do you have to say of the interpretation that the *rock* is *Christ?*

173. Of the interpretation that the *rock* is *the faith and confession of Peter?*

174. What is the *third* interpretation of this passage?

175. What does Bengel say of this interpretation?

176. Meyer?

177. What may be said of this interpretation?

178. Show that the Roman Church cannot adduce for their interpretation the *unanimous* consent of the Fathers.

179. What conclusions may we therefore reach with reference to the Roman theory of the Primacy and Jurisdiction of Peter?

180. What have you to say of Peter's Episcopacy at Rome?

181. What does Littledale say of the evidence of the Petrine claims?

182. What is the real basis of this position of the Roman Church?

183. Why cannot we rely on this statement?

184. When is this claim of the episcopate of Peter first clearly brought forward?

185. Show that Peter the Apostle could not have been a bishop.

186. Show that the bishop of Rome is not Peter's successor.

187. What difficulty arises in claiming that the bishop of Rome succeeded to the supposed primacy of Peter?

188. When did the Church first speak of a visible head?

189. Trace the development of the claims of the bishops of Rome.

190. What is the origin of the idea of any kind of primacy?

191. Show that this Roman primacy was positively rejected by the Council of Calcedon (451 A. D.).

192. What testimony does a Roman Catholic writer bear to this whole question of Papal authority?

193. What do you have to say of the doctrine of Papal Infallibilty?

194. Show from history that the Popes were not infallible.

195. What do you know of Abelard's work *Sic et Non?*

196. Of the doctrine of the Immaculate Conception of the Virgin Mary?

197. What testimony have we concerning the character of the Popes during the tenth century?

198. What theories have been held with reference to this infallibility of the Church?

199. How adroitly was this managed at the meeting of the Vatican Council in 1870?

200. What do you have to say of the continued *Inspiration* theory of the Roman Church?

201. What do you have to say, in general, of the Roman marks of the Church?

202. Of the name *Catholic?*

203. Of their mark *antiquity?*

204. Of their mark *abiding duration?*

205. Of their mark *succession of bishops?*

206. Of their mark *apostolicity?*

207. Of their mark *being under the Jurisdiction of the Pope?*

208. Show that even in the Church of Rome there has been no true external unity.

209. Discuss their mark *sanctity of doctrine.*

209. Their mark *efficacy of doctrine.*

210. Their mark *sanctity of life.*

211. What may be said of the marks brought forward by Bellarmine.

III. *The Protestant Church*

212. In what does the weak point of Protestantism lie?

213. On what did the leaders of the two branches of Protestantism divide?

214. How did Rome take advantage of this?

215. In what, in general, does the cause of Protestant divisions lie?

216. What was the first main point on which the Lutheran and Reformed theologians differed?

217. How did this influence practical life?

218. In what sense may we compare Protestantism with Romanism?

219. How does the Lutheran Church state her fundamental principle on this point?

220. What is the second main point on which the Lutheran and Reformed Churches differ?

IV. *Lutheran Protestanism*

221. Name the Confessional Books of the Lutheran Church.

222. In what part is the doctrine of the Church discussed?

223. Of what does Art. VII. of A.C. treat?

224. Give a brief analysis of Art. VII.

225. Of what does Art. VIII. treat?

226. Give a brief analysis.

227. Under what two headings does the Apology discuss Art. VII?

228. Give an analysis of the discussion on the definition of the Church.

229. Of the discussion on the unity of the Church.

230. Give an analysis of the Apology on Art. VIII.

231. Give an analysis of the discussion in the Snialcald Articles on the Church.

232. Of the discussion in the Large Catechism.

233. Of the discussion in the Formula of Concord.

V. *Lecture on Art. VII. of Augsburg Confession*

234. What two things are necessary for the true unity of the Church?

235. Explain Eph. 4:5.

236. What four great lessons can we learn from Matt. 28:18–20?

237. Prove that this passage and Art. VII. of A. C. teach the same doctrine.

238. Against what two antithetical errors does the N.T. doctrine of Baptism guard?

239. Prove from Scripture that Baptism rightly administered is a necessary characteristic of the one Church.

240. Show that the Lord's Supper is an essential mark of the true unity of the Church.

241. What two things are involved in a right administration of a Sacrament?

242. Discuss more fully the idea that the organic center of the unity of the Church lies in her faith.

243. Show that the Confessors define very carefully what is necessary to the *true unity* of the Church.

244. Show that this unity does not depend on the similarity of *human traditions*.

245. Nor on similarity of *human ceremonies*.

246. Define Ritualism.

247. Discuss Ritualism in an unfavorable sense.

248. What is the position of the Lutheran Church on these points?

249. Why does the Lutheran Church lay so much stress on *unity of doctrine*.

250. "What is the first thing necessary to bring about the unity of doctrine?

251. What is the second step?

VI. *The Teaching of our Older Dogmaticians*

252. What was Luther's earliest definition of the Church?

253. What later definition of his is more in accordance with Scripture?

254. Present in brief Luther's teaching concerning the Church.

255. What aspect of the Church was emphasized in opposition to the Romanists?

256. In opposition to the Anabaptists.

257. What is the teaching of Melanchthon?

258. Upon what aspect of the Church did Chemnitz lay stress?

259. How does Hutter define the Church?

260. Distinguish between the visible and the invisible Church.

261. Give the best definition of the Church.

262. How does Quenstedt prove from Scripture that the Church is, "the congregation of saints?"

263. Distinguish between the militant and the triumphant Church.

264. How does Hollaz establish the *unity* of the Church?

265. How does Gerhard develop the *holiness* of the Church?

266. How does Hollaz discuss the *Catholicity* of the Church?

267. The *Apostolicity* of the Church?

268. What is meant by the phrase "out of the Church is no salvation?"

269. What does Gerhard say on this point?

270. In what sense is the Church universal?

271. What is meant by a particular Church?

272. Discuss the topic more fully.

273. Distinguish between a *pure* and an *impure* Church.

274. Show that the falseness of a Church is a relative thing.

275. In what sense may we speak of the purity of a Church as relative?

276. Why is salvation possible even in some of the false or impure churches?

277. What are the marks of a true Church?

278. How can we determine whether the doctrine of a Church is pure?

279. What value do the works of standard theologians have?

280. Discuss briefly Lutheranism versus Romanism.

281. Discuss briefly the relation of Lutheranism to Protestantism.

281 *a.* What is meant by the Synthetic Church?

282. What is meant by the Representative Church?

283. How does Quenstedt present this matter?

284. Buddeus?

285. Show how far this representative character may be developed.

VII. *The Later Development of the Doctrine of the Church*

286. What was the nature of this development?

287. What was the influence of Spener?

288. Of Rationalism?

289. Of Supernaturalism?

290. Of Kant?

291. Of Schleiermacher?

292. Of Hegel?

293. Of Rothe?

294. What was the tendency of the later development?

295. What does Dorner say of the invisibility of the Church?

296. Of her visibility?

297. Of what value is this distinction between the *visible* and *invisible* Church?

298. How does Martensen distinguish between the *formal* and *material* principle of Protestantism?

299. How does he distinguish between Lutheran and Reformed Protestantism?

300. What general position with reference to the Church did Stahl, Vilmar, and Loehe, take?

301. What theologians are known as the Erlangen School?

302. What general position did these theologians take?

303. What view did Grabau and the Buffalo Synod take?

304. What view was taken by Dr. Walther?

305. What position was taken by the German Iowa Synod?

VIII. *Theories of Church Government*

306. Name the four leading theories.

307. Define the Roman Catholic view.

308. In what does the Eastern Church differ?

309. The Old Catholics?

310. State the High-Church Anglican view.

311. State the Low-Church Anglican view.

312. What position does the Reformed Episcopal Church

313. What do you have to say of Methodist Episcopacy?

314. Of Moravian Episcopacy?

315. Of Lutheran Episcopacy?

316. Define the Presbyterian Polity.

317. Who first put it into practical application?

318. Give an account of its growth and influence.

319. Describe the Congregational Polity.

320. Distinguish between English and American Congregationalism.

321. What Polity do the Baptists favor?

322. Show that the Church Polity of the Lutheran Church in this country is largely Presbyterian.

323. Show that some Synods are largely congregational.

IX. *Constitution of the Church in Apostolic Times*

324. What is the object of Ecclesiastical Polity?

325. Prove that bishops and presbyters were identical in the

326. What do we learn from Clement of Rome?

327. Why is there no evidence in the N.T. for a *Jus divinum* diocesan Episcopacy.

328. Nor for a *Jus divinum* lay presbyterial office?

329. Show that the diaconate was the first office established in the Church.

330. Give an account of their election.

331. What were their functions?

332. Show that they were aids of the minister.

333. Discuss the diaconate more fully.

334. Discuss the female diaconate.

335. Whence did the office of *elder* take its name and origin?

336. Whence did the word *bishop* have its origin?

337. What were the duties of the presbyters or bishops?

338. Trace the development of Church Government in the Gentile Churches.

X. *The Development of the Episcopal Hierarchy*

339. Trace the origin of the Congregational Episcopate.

340. Trace the origin of the Diocesan Episcopate.

341. With what three great names is the development of the Episcopacy connected?

342. Where do we find the minutes of the first Council of the Christian Church recorded?

343. What facts can we learn from this record?

344. Why were Synods soon held regularly?

345. What important facts do we learn from the history of the early Councils?

346. Show how finally an Ecumenical Council was held.

347. Name the eight earliest Ecumenical Councils, and give dates.

348. Trace the origin of the Metropolitan constitution.

349. Trace the steps by which the Roman hierarchial form of government was developed.

350. What was the relation of the Church to the Civil Orders?

351. Sketch briefly Church Polity during the Middle Ages.

XI. *Church Polity of the Reformation Period*

352. In what way did the doctrine of the Reformation influence Church Polity?

353. Discuss the topic of the universal priesthood.

354. What, in the judgment of the Reformers, was the great significance of the ministry?

355. What view was taken of the pastor's office?

356. What was the nature of the Church constitution thus developed?

357. Why are the teachings of the Lutheran Confessions important on this point?

358. Under what six points may Art. XXVIII. of *Augsburg Confession, of Ecclesiastical power,* be analyzed?

359. Discuss briefly its presentation of the Scripture doctrine.

360. How do they limit the Jurisdiction of Bishops?

361. What do they teach concerning their power to institute human ordinances?

362. Give a brief outline of *Apology* on Art. XIV., *of Ecclesiastical Orders.*

362. Of *Apology* on Art. XV., *of Human Traditions in the Church.*

363. Of Apology on Art. XXVIII., *of Ecclesiastical Power.*

364. What does the *Apology* teach concerning the power of the bishops?

365. Of traditions?

366. How do they answer the arguments of Rome?

367. What do the *Smalcald Articles* teach *of the Keys?*

368. *Of Excommunication?*

369. Under what six points is *the Power and Jurisdiction of Bishops* discussed in the Appendix?

370. On what occasion did Luther more fully develop the doctrine of the universal priesthood?

371. Give an outline of his earlier teaching on the Church.

372. Give a summary of his later teaching.

373. What, in general, may be said of Luther's teaching on the Church?

374. Summarize the teaching of Melanchthon.

375. What is meant by the doctrine of the Three Estates?

376. What is meant by the *Episcopal* System in the Lutheran Church?

377. Who developed this system?

378. Define the *Territorial* System.

379. Who developed this system?

380. Define the *Collegial* System.

381. Under what influence was this developed?

382. What can you say of the relation of the Lutheran Church to the State?

XII. *Studies in Lutheran Church Polity*

383. Why is the study of Church Polity so important at present?

384. Why is the Church Polity of the Lutheran Church in such an undeveloped state?

385. Why is this subject of such importance now?

386. Why are there such diverse tendencies in Church Polity in the Lutheran Church?

387. What form of Church Polity ought to be encouraged?

388. Why is it so important that the congregational life be brought into greater activity?

389. How ought a congregation to be organized in the mutual relations of pastors, deacons, and congregation proper?

390. What is the truest view of the pastor's relation to his flock?

391. Why is it not wise for the individual congregation to make regulations concerning the general confession and the general order of the Church?

XIII. *The Church Polity of the General Council*

392. Who has supreme power over the Church?

393. What power has Christ committed to the Church?

394. *What* is *just* power exercised by the Church?

395. When does the Church exercise *unjust* power?

396. What three things are involved in *just* power?

397. Through what instrument does the Church exercise *just* power?

398. Distinguish between *the power of the order* and *the power of the keys.*

399. What is the absolute guide of the Church in the exercise of her power?

400. What are the primary bodies through which this power is normally exercised?

401. Define a congregation in the normal state.

402. What is the nature of ordinary Church power?

403. Distinguish between *abnormal* and *normal* exercise of Church power.

404. Name four false theories of Church power.

405. What is meant by *a representative?*

406. How far does his act bind the principal?

407. Show that a congregation can be ruled in no way but *representatively.*

408. In what way do representatives act for their principals?

409. To whom does the power to call ministers rightly belong?

410. Distinguish between the universal priesthood and the ministerial office.

411. In what way does the pastor of a congregation become their representative?

412. Illustrate it in the case of the representative system of our own country.

413. Of whom is every minister a representative?

414. What do you have to say of lay-delegates?

415. Of Ruling Elders *and Jus divinum* lay-eldership?

416. What were the deacons of the Early Church?

417. Why do we insist on congregational representation?

418. Show that the judgments of Synods are the judgments of the Church?

419. Why has an individual congregation not the same authority as a Synod?

420. Why are congregations the lowest Church authority in all questions not strictly congregational?

421. Show that a free General Council or Synod, chosen by the Church, is representatively the Church itself.

422. What must be the marks of a true representative Council or Synod?

423. What is meant by the *Synthetic* Church?

424. By the Representative Church?

425. To what limit may *representation* go?

426. For whom especially are constitutions prepared?

427. Under what circumstances may a Synod withdraw from a General body?

428. Explain and qualify the statement, the form of Lutheran Church Government is that of *a pure monarchy*.

429. Show that her government is *not a hierarchy*.

430. Show that it is not an *aristocracy*.

431. Nor a sporadic *Polyarchy* like Congregationalism.

432. What is the best name given to her ideal form of government?

433. Show that it is *Christocratic*.

434. Show that it is *representative* and *elective*.

435. Show that it is *real* and *decisive*, if rightly applied.

436. Why have we a right to assume that the decisions of Synods are more likely to be true and right than those of single congregations?

437. Show that the admission of fallibility does not destroy rightful authority.

438. What objections have been raised against accepting the decisions of Synods?

439. Show that the authority claimed for Synods is not in conflict with the right of minorities.

440. Show that this is true, even if it should happen that a minority be in the right.

441. Show that there is such a thing as authority even if it prove to be fallible.

442. Why can we not refer questions, decided by general bodies, for decision to individual congregations?

443. How may congregations protect their rights?

444. What is the duty of a delegate appointed to represent a congregation?

445. For what objects ought Synods to be organized?

446. What position does Stahl take?

447. What position is represented by Walther?

448. State the first three theses laid down by Walther.

449. Criticise Walther's *sixth* thesis.

450. Criticise his *seventh* thesis.

451. How does Stahl criticise these last two theses?

452. To whom, according to Walther, was *the power of the Keys* given?

453. How does Stahl criticise this exegesis?

454. What other difficulty arises in adopting Walther's position?

455. How does Stahl criticise Walther's view of the organization of the N.T. Church?

456. What credit does Stahl give to Walther?

457. How does he, in general, criticise the tendency of Missouri?

458. What is the weakness of Stahl's position?

459. What has been the praiseworthy aim of Missouri?

460. In what does the weakness of their whole system lie?

461. What lamentable mistake have they made in the matter of historical scholarship?

XIV. *Literature*

462. Name some valuable General Works bearing on the *Church*.

463. Name the best works in which the history of the doctrine of the Church is discussed.

464. Name the best General Doctrinal Works from the Baptist point of view.

464. By Congregational theologians.

465. By theologians of the Dutch Reformed Church.

466. By scholars of the Church of England (Episcopal).

467. Of the German Reformed Church.

468. Name two of the most prominent of the Mediating Lutheran, theologians.

469. Name ten works by strictly Confessional Lutherans.

470. Name some of the most prominent Methodist theologians.

471. Name some of the great Presbyterian writers on Dogmatics.

472. Name some important Roman Catholic works.

473. Name some of the more important Anglican works on the Church and Church Polity.

474. Name some of the best works on Congregationalism.

475. On Lutheran Protestantism.

476. On Presbyterianism.

477. On Roman Catholicism.